GRADE **5**

Review

Find the answers.

①
$$\begin{array}{r} 2908 \\ + 1374 \\ \hline 3282 \end{array}$$

②
$$\begin{array}{r} 324 \\ \times \quad 6 \\ \hline 1944 \end{array}$$

③
$$\begin{array}{r} 6843 \\ - \quad 123 \\ \hline 6720 \end{array}$$

④
$$\begin{array}{r} 75 \\ 5\overline{)375} \\ 35 \times \\ \hline 25 \end{array}$$

⑤
$$\begin{array}{r} 3856 \\ - \quad 298 \\ \hline 3558 \end{array}$$

⑥
$$\begin{array}{r} 1296 \\ + 2345 \\ \hline 3641 \end{array}$$

⑦ 868 ÷ 4 = _____

⑧ 412 x 7 = _____

⑨ 1000 x 8 = _____

⑩ 9 x 100 = _____

Quick Tip

To multiply a number by 10, 100, ..., just add 1, 2, ... zeros to the number.

Fill in the missing numbers in the patterns.

⑪ 10, 20, 30, __40__, __50__, __60__, __70__, __80__, __90__, __100__

⑫ 3, 6, 9, __12__, __15__, __18__, __21__, __24__, __27__, __30__

⑬ 9, 18, 27, __36__, __45__, __54__, __63__, __72__, __81__, __90__

⑭ 7, 14, 21, __28__, __35__, __42__, __49__, __56__, __63__, __70__

⑮ 15, 30, 45, ____, ____, ____, ____, ____, ____, ____

$$\begin{array}{r} 15 \\ + 6 \\ \hline 90 \end{array}$$

Use the patterns above to find the products.

⑯ 6 x 7 = __42__

⑰ 8 x 3 = __24__

⑱ 5 x 10 = __56__

⑲ 9 x 6 = __54__

⑳ 7 x 8 = __56__

㉑ 8 x 9 = __72__

㉒ 7 x 9 = __63__

㉓ 8 x 10 = __80__

㉔ 8 x 15 = __120__

㉕ 15 x 6 = __90__

Quick Tip

Even if the order of multiplication has changed, the product is still the same,
e.g. 3 x 9 = 9 x 3 = 27

$$\begin{array}{r} 4,15 \\ 8 \\ \hline 120 \end{array}$$

2

Find the answers.

㉖ 7 x 8 = 56 56 ÷ 8 = 7	㉗ 6 x 5 = 30 30 ÷ 6 = 5	㉘ 72 ÷ 9 = 8 8 x 9 = ______
㉙ 98 + 2 = 100 100 – 2 = 98	㉚ 24 – 16 = 8 8 + 16 = 24	㉛ 123 ÷ 3 = 41 41 x 3 = ______
㉜ 56 + 48 = 104 104 – 56 = 48	㉝ 83 – 38 = 45 83 – 45 = 38	㉞ 112 ÷ 8 = 14 112 ÷ 14 = ______

Fill in the missing numbers.

㉟ 2 + 8 = 10	㊱ 25 – ______ = 21
㊲ 17 + 8 = 25	㊳ 21 – ______ = 15
㊴ 15 – 7 = 8	㊵ ______ + 7 = 20
㊶ 123 – 4 = 119	㊷ ______ + 120 = 150
㊸ 20 – 8 = 12	㊹ ______ + 130 = 149
㊺ 16 + 25 = 41	㊻ ______ – 110 = 28

Add or subtract.

㊼ 2.9 + 3.1 = ______	㊽ 5.9 – 1.7 = ______
㊾ 3.8 + 2.7 = ______	㊿ 9.2 – 5.6 = ______
(51) 16.1 – 4.5 = ______	(52) 23.6 + 8.9 = ______
(53) 37.4 – 12.6 = ______	(54) 11.4 + 45.7 = ______
(55) 230 + 51.7 = ______	(56) 182 – 23.9 = ______
(57) 7.4 + 26 = ______	(58) 41 – 9.8 = ______
(59) 87 – 34.9 = ______	(60) 31.6 + 57.5 = ______

The children are eating pizzas. See how much each child eats and solve the problems.

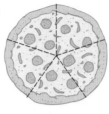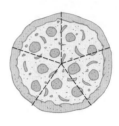

Paul eats $\frac{3}{5}$ of a pizza. Stan eats $\frac{2}{5}$ of a pizza. Steve eats $\frac{4}{5}$ of a pizza. Sue eats $\frac{1}{5}$ of a pizza.

㉑ Who eats the most pizza? _____

㉒ Who eats the least pizza? _____

㉓ If they have 2 pizzas, will there be any pizza left over? _____

㉔ Put the children in order from the child who eats the most pizza to the one who eats the least.

_____ , _____ , _____ , _____

Complete the chart below.

Fraction	㉕	㉖	$\frac{1}{4}$	$\frac{2}{5}$	$\frac{3}{10}$	$\frac{37}{100}$
Decimal	0.9	0.04	㉗	㉘	㉙	㉚

Write the decimals to the nearest hundredth at which the javelins land.

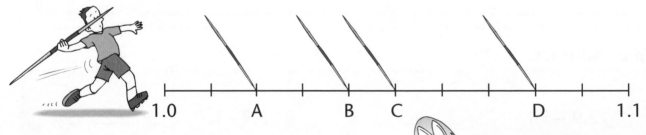

㉛ A = _____   ㉜ B = _____

㉝ C = _____   ㉞ D = _____

Quick Tip

Divide one tenth (0.1) into 10 equal parts. Each part is one hundredth (0.01).

one   1.03   one and one tenth

1.0   1.1

10 equal parts

Write a fraction to represent the shaded part in each question.

㉟

㊱  _____

㊲ _____

Solve the problems.

⑱ Paul buys a 70¢ chocolate bar. He pays $1.00. How
    much change does he get? $ _____

⑲ Pat pays a toonie for a $1.50 sandwich. How much
    change does he get?   _____ ¢

⑳ Sarah has $32.75 in her piggy bank. How much does
    she have if her mom gives her $15.50 more? $ _____

㉑ A pair of jeans costs $52.50. Peggy has only $45.75.
    How much more does she need to pay for the jeans? $ _____

㉒ Sam bought a $1.85 hamburger and a $1.90 milkshake
    for his lunch. How much did his lunch cost? $ _____

What transformation is used to get each image? Write translation, reflection or rotation.

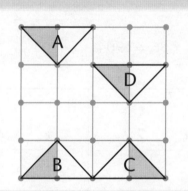

㉓ A → B _____

㉔ A → C _____

㉕ A → D _____

㉖ B → C _____

Find the perimeter and area of each shape.

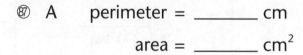

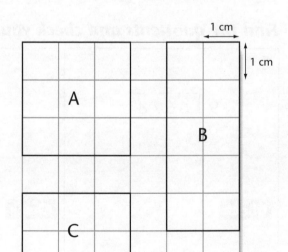

㉗ A   perimeter = _____ cm

           area = _____ cm^2

㉘ B   perimeter = _____ cm

           area = _____ cm^2

㉙ C   perimeter = _____ cm

           area = _____ cm^2

5

1 Operations with Whole Numbers

Find the sums or differences.

①	②
3098 1230 + 4362	3408 1290 + 2671

Quick Tip

When doing addition, don't forget to add the digit carried over from the right column. When doing subtraction, remember to borrow 10 from the left column if you can't take away.

③	④	⑤	⑥
2000 – 1098	5298 – 1084	4287 – 1999	4753 – 2398

Find the products.

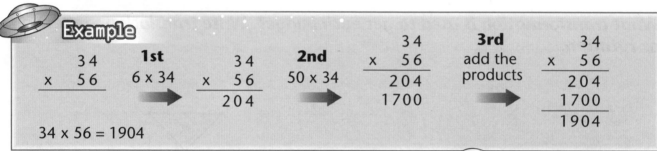

Example

	1st		2nd		3rd	
34 x 56	6 x 34	34 x 56 204	50 x 34	34 x 56 204 1700	add the products	34 x 56 204 1700 1904

34 x 56 = 1904

⑦	⑧	⑨
54 x 27	38 x 49	17 x 65

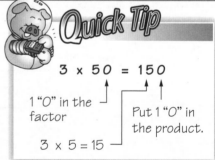

Quick Tip

3 x 50 = 150

1 "0" in the factor

Put 1 "0" in the product.

3 x 5 = 15

Find the quotients and check your answers by multiplication and addition.

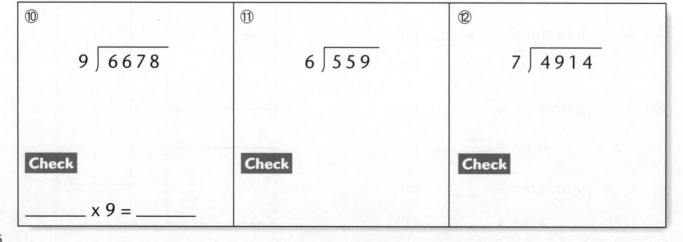

⑩	⑪	⑫
9 ⟌ 6678	6 ⟌ 559	7 ⟌ 4914
Check	**Check**	**Check**
____ x 9 = ____		

What is the message? Do the division and match the letters with the remainders.

⑬ 1235 ÷ 2   Remainder = _____   **W**

⑭ 3472 ÷ 5   Remainder = _____   **L**

⑮ 7560 ÷ 3   Remainder = _____   **N**

⑯ 1679 ÷ 8   Remainder = _____   **E**

⑰ 2879 ÷ 9   Remainder = _____   **O**

⑱ 5433 ÷ 6   Remainder = _____   **D**

⑲ 1621 ÷ 7   Remainder = _____   **G**

⑳ 2129 ÷ 6   Remainder = _____   **R**

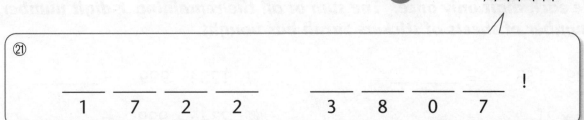

㉑

___ ___ ___ ___   ___ ___ ___ ___ !
 1   7   2   2   3   8   0   7

Do the calculations mentally. Put a check mark ✔ in the box if the answer is correct; otherwise, write the correct answer in the box.

㉒ 2 x 10 x 7   = _140_ ☐   ㉓ 200 ÷ 10 ÷ 5   = _4_ ☐

㉔ 35 − 8 + 7   = _20_ ☐   ㉕ 78 + 12 − 20   = _70_ ☐

㉖ 300 ÷ 30 x 2   = _5_ ☐   ㉗ 99 ÷ 9 x 2   = _22_ ☐

㉘ 100 x 2 ÷ 200   = _1_ ☐   ㉙ 124 ÷ 2 x 6   = _372_ ☐

㉚ 5000 ÷ 50 ÷ 100   = _10_ ☐

㉛ 400 ÷ 100 X 5   = _200_ ☐

㉜ 540 − 240 − 100 − 150 = _150_ ☐

㉝ 324 − 24 + 224   = _524_ ☐

 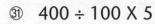

Quick Tip

Do (+ and −) or (x and ÷) in order from left to right. Simplify the division by deleting the same number of zeros from the dividend and divisor,

e.g. 2000 ÷ 20 = 200 ÷ 2 = 100

Write the answers in numerals.

㉞ Mandy has one thousand three hundred four beads. Jane has two thousand seven hundred twenty-one beads. How many beads do Jane and Mandy have in all? ________ beads

㉟ How many more beads does Jane have than Mandy? ________ beads

㊱ Mandy has 324 green beads. How many of Mandy's beads are not green? ________ beads

㊲ Jane has 456 green beads. How many of Jane's beads are not green? ________ beads

㊳ How many green beads do Jane and Mandy have in all? ________ beads

Calculate and shade the answers in the number puzzle horizontally or vertically. Shade each digit only once. The sum of all the remaining 1-digit numbers is the number of sheets of stickers Sarah has bought.

㊴ 239 – 158 = ________

㊵ 1234 – 999 = ________

㊶ 58 x 21 = ________

㊷ 2345 + 999 = ________

㊸ 1080 ÷ 9 = ________

㊹ 15 x 14 = ________

㊺ 3456 + 1398 = ________

㊻ 1981 – 1973 = ________

㊼ 17 x 11 = ________

㊽ 203 ÷ 7 = ________

㊾ 576 ÷ 8 = ________

㊿

2	3	5	1	8	7
5	1	2	1	8	4
7	2	3	1	1	8
2	9	8	2	2	5
0	7	1	0	1	4
3	3	4	4	0	8

(51) Sum = ________

(52) Sarah has bought ________ sheets of stickers.

Brad and Pat go swimming. Solve the problems and show your work.

㊾ Brad takes 90 seconds to swim one length of the pool. How long does he take to swim 12 lengths?

He takes _____ seconds to swim 12 lengths.

㊾ Pat takes 75 seconds to swim one length. How long does he take to swim 15 lengths?

㊾ Brad swims 12 lengths and Pat swims 15 lengths. What is the difference between their times?

㊾ During the first 7 days of August, 1848 swimmers used the pool. What was the average number of swimmers per day?

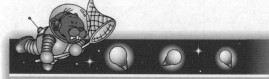

MIND BOGGLER

Who swims farther? You may use a calculator.

Refer to questions ㊾ and ㊾. How many lengths of the pool can Brad and Pat each swim in 1 hour?

Brad can swim _____ lengths. Pat can swim _____ lengths.

Quick Tip

1 hour = 60 minutes
1 minute = 60 seconds

2 Fractions

Example

Dan cuts a pizza into 6 slices.
He eats 2 slices.

He eats $\frac{2}{6}$ of the pizza.

Dan's cutting

John cuts the same pizza into 3 slices.
He eats 1 slice.

He eats $\frac{1}{3}$ of the pizza.

Dan and John eat the same amount.

$$\frac{2}{6} = \frac{1}{3}$$

$\frac{2}{6}$ and $\frac{1}{3}$ are equivalent fractions.

John's cutting

Complete the equivalent fractions by filling in the missing numerators or denominators.

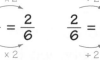 **Quick Tip**

$$\frac{1}{3} \xrightarrow{\times 2} \frac{2}{6} \qquad \frac{2}{6} \xrightarrow{\div 2} \frac{1}{3}$$

$\frac{1}{3}$ and $\frac{2}{6}$ are equivalent fractions.
Multiply or divide both the numerator and denominator by the same number to get an equivalent fraction.

$\frac{1}{3}$ is in lowest terms since the only number that can divide both the denominator and the numerator is 1.

① $\frac{1}{4} = \frac{}{8}$

② $\frac{1}{2} = \frac{}{4}$

③ $\frac{6}{9} = \frac{}{3}$

④ $\frac{8}{} = \frac{4}{7}$

⑤ $\frac{10}{25} = \frac{2}{}$

⑥ $\frac{5}{15} = \frac{}{3}$

Match each fraction with its lowest terms. Write the letter in the circle.

⑦ $\frac{10}{12}$ ⑧ $\frac{18}{21}$ ⑨ $\frac{3}{15}$ ⑩ $\frac{6}{8}$ ⑪ $\frac{6}{10}$ ⑫ $\frac{6}{9}$

A) $\frac{2}{3}$ B) $\frac{1}{5}$ C) $\frac{3}{4}$ D) $\frac{3}{5}$ E) $\frac{5}{6}$ F) $\frac{6}{7}$

Colour the diagrams to show the fractions. Circle the larger fractions.

⑬ $\frac{1}{3}$
$\frac{1}{4}$

⑭ $\frac{1}{2}$
$\frac{2}{5}$

⑮ $\frac{2}{3}$
$\frac{3}{4}$

Example

Put $\dfrac{2}{3}$, $\dfrac{3}{4}$, $\dfrac{1}{2}$ in order from least to greatest using <.

$$\dfrac{2}{3} = \dfrac{2 \times 4}{3 \times 4} = \dfrac{8}{12} \qquad \dfrac{3}{4} = \dfrac{3 \times 3}{4 \times 3} = \dfrac{9}{12} \qquad \dfrac{1}{2} = \dfrac{1 \times 6}{2 \times 6} = \dfrac{6}{12}$$

$$\dfrac{1}{2} < \dfrac{2}{3} < \dfrac{3}{4}$$

Write True (T) or False (F) for each statement.

⑯ $\dfrac{3}{4} < \dfrac{4}{5}$ (T)   ⑰ $\dfrac{7}{8} = \dfrac{14}{16}$ (F)   ⑱ $\dfrac{7}{6} > 1\dfrac{1}{2}$ (F)

⑲ $\dfrac{2}{3} > \dfrac{2}{5}$ (F)   ⑳ $\dfrac{1}{9} < \dfrac{1}{10}$ (T)   ㉑ $\dfrac{12}{24} = \dfrac{10}{20}$ (T)

㉒ $\dfrac{5}{6} = \dfrac{7}{8}$ (F)   ㉓ $\dfrac{7}{6} > \dfrac{2}{3}$ (T)   ㉔ $\dfrac{13}{3} > \dfrac{13}{2}$ (T)

㉕ $\dfrac{15}{20} > \dfrac{9}{12}$ (F)   ㉖ $\dfrac{14}{60} = \dfrac{4}{15}$ (F)   ㉗ $3\dfrac{1}{8} < 3\dfrac{1}{4}$ (F)

Order the fractions from greatest to least using >.

Quick Tip

Convert a mixed number to an improper fraction:

$$4\dfrac{1}{3} = \dfrac{4 \times 3 + 1}{3} = \dfrac{13}{3}$$

Convert an improper fraction to a mixed number:

$$\dfrac{13}{3} = 4\dfrac{1}{3}$$
$$\begin{array}{r} 4 \\ 3\overline{\smash)13} \\ \underline{12} \\ 1 \end{array}$$

㉘ $2\dfrac{1}{5} \qquad \dfrac{11}{4} \qquad \dfrac{5}{2}$

_____

㉙ $\dfrac{6}{4} \qquad \dfrac{7}{8} \qquad \dfrac{7}{4}$

_____

㉚ $3\dfrac{1}{3} \qquad 3\dfrac{1}{6} \qquad \dfrac{13}{4}$

_____

㉛ $\dfrac{3}{4} \qquad \dfrac{4}{3} \qquad \dfrac{13}{3}$

_____

Write each fraction in lowest terms and as a decimal.

Examples

 $\dfrac{1}{10} = 0.1$ $\dfrac{5}{10} = 0.5$ $\dfrac{1}{100} = 0.01$ 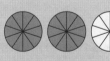 $\dfrac{21}{10} = 2\dfrac{1}{10} = 2.1$

		$\dfrac{6}{10}$	$\dfrac{85}{100}$	$\dfrac{54}{100}$	$\dfrac{36}{100}$	$\dfrac{75}{100}$	$\dfrac{38}{10}$	$\dfrac{15}{10}$
㉜	Fraction in lowest terms							
㉝	Decimal							

Solve the problems.   Give the fractions in lowest terms.

㉞ In a fruit bowl, there are 2 bananas, 1 pear and 3 apples. The fruits are divided equally among 4 children.

    a. Write the fraction of each kind of fruit each child gets.

        _____ of a banana   _____ of a pear   _____ of an apple

    b. Write the fractions in order from least to greatest using <.

    _____

㉟ On Halloween, Dan collects 9 chocolate bars.

    a. If he divides the chocolate bars equally between himself and his brother, each gets _____ bars.

    b. If he divides them equally among 6 children, each gets _____ bars.

    c. If he divides them equally among 4 children, each gets _____ bars.

㊱ In Mrs. Ling's class, there are 30 students.

    a. $\frac{2}{5}$ of the students are girls. There are _____ girls in the class.

    b. On Friday $\frac{1}{6}$ of the students are away. _____ students are not in the class on Friday.

    c. 9 children go home for lunch. What fraction of the children stay at school for lunch?

    _____

    d. Can Mrs. Ling divide the class into 4 equal groups? Explain.

    _____

    _____

Quick Tip

Divide 30 students into 5 groups. Each group has 6 students.

$\frac{1}{5}$ of 30 is 6.

There are 12 children at Ali's party. Help Ali solve the problems.

③⑦ The children will play in the garden for $\frac{1}{2}$ hour, watch a video for $\frac{3}{5}$ hour, and have snacks for $\frac{3}{4}$ hour.

a. Which activity will take the longest time? _____

b. Which activity will take the least time? _____

③⑧ 3 pizzas are divided equally among 12 children. How much pizza does each child get? Give your answer in two equivalent fractions.

_____ of a pizza

_____ of a pizza

③⑨ There are 4 bottles of pop. How much pop can each child have?

_____ bottle

④⓪ The birthday cake is divided into 16 equal slices. If each child eats 1 slice, what fraction of the cake is left over?

_____ of the cake

④① Ali receives some storybooks for his birthday. He puts them on the bookshelf. Now there are 100 books in all on the shelf. If only 18 of the books belong to Ali, write a decimal to represent the fraction of books that belong to him.

_____ of the books

④② Ali gets 10 gifts. 3 of the gifts are books and 5 are board games. Write a decimal to represent each kind of gift.

a. Books _____

b. Board games _____

c. Neither books nor board games _____

MIND BOGGLER

Who has more books?

$\frac{3}{5}$ of 40 books are mine.

Kevin

0.35 of 100 books are mine.

$\frac{35}{100}$

Jane

Kevin has more books.

3 Decimals

Add or subtract the decimals.

Quick Tip

Remember to align the decimal points when doing vertical addition or subtraction. Don't forget to put a decimal point in the answer.

①
```
  5.43
+ 2.08
```

②
```
  7.84
+ 1.16
```

③
```
  3.09
+ 0.97
```

④
```
  8.97
- 1.45
```

⑤
```
  5.69
- 2.81
```

⑥
```
  6.23
- 3.85
```

⑦ $12.23 + 8.98$ = _____

⑧ $23.45 - 2.93$ = _____

⑨ $82.36 - 35.47$ = _____

⑩ $21.98 + 27.09$ = _____

⑪ $38.46 + 0.91$ = _____

⑫ $42.38 - 0.92$ = _____

⑬ $55.55 - 16.87$ = _____

⑭ $41.63 - 7.9$ = _____

Complete each of the following statements by filling in the fractions with denominators of 10 or 100.

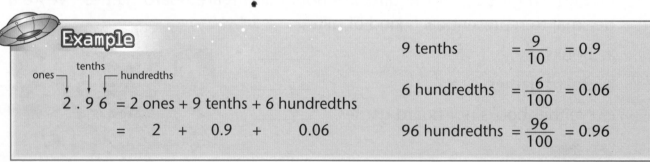

Example

ones — tenths — hundredths

2.96 = 2 ones + 9 tenths + 6 hundredths

= 2 + 0.9 + 0.06

9 tenths $= \frac{9}{10}$ = 0.9

6 hundredths $= \frac{6}{100}$ = 0.06

96 hundredths $= \frac{96}{100}$ = 0.96

⑮ 0.07 = _____

⑯ 0.49 $= \frac{4}{10} +$ _____ = _____

⑰ 0.7 $= \frac{}{100} = \frac{}{10}$

⑱ 0.79 = _____ $+ \frac{9}{100}$ = _____

⑲ $0.6 + 0.05$ = _____

⑳ $0.3 + 0.04$ = _____

㉑ $123.45 = 100 + 20 + 3 +$ _____ + _____

Examples

① 15.98 x 3 = ?

```
    1 5 . 9 8
  x       3
  ─────────────
    4 7 . 9 4
```

same number of decimal places

Write the decimal point in the product.

15.98 x 3 = 47.94

② 32.9 ÷ 5 = ?

```
        6 . 5 8
    5 ) 3 2 . 9 0
        3 0
        ─────
          2 9
          2 5
          ─────
            4 0
            4 0
```

Decimal point in the quotient is directly above the one in the dividend.

Add zero to the right of the dividend and continue to divide until the remainder is zero or you have enough decimal places.

32.9 ÷ 5 = 6.58

Find the products.

㉒	㉓	㉔	㉕
6.8 x 4	3.7 x 5	20.15 x 9	9.04 x 3

㉖ 17.41 x 7 = _____

㉗ 0.93 x 6 = _____

㉘ 24.09 x 8 = _____

㉙ 18.75 x 2 = _____

Estimate and check ✔ the correct products. Cross ✘ the incorrect ones.

㉚ 5.07 x 2 = <u>10.14</u> ◯

㉛ 15.18 x 5 = <u>65.90</u> ◯

㉜ 0.93 x 7 = <u>65.1</u> ◯

㉝ 21.8 x 8 = <u>11.44</u> ◯

㉞ 6.98 x 6 = <u>41.88</u> ◯

㉟ 2.34 x 9 = <u>210.6</u> ◯

Quick Tip

Round each decimal to the nearest whole number to do estimation. Make sure that the product has the same number of decimal places as the factor.

Find the quotients.

㊱	㊲	㊳
7) 51.1	4) 25.16	5) 19.9

㊴ 73.86 ÷ 6 = _____

㊵ 70.8 ÷ 8 = _____

㊶ 13.5 ÷ 2 = _____

Do the estimation by rounding each dividend to the closest whole number that is divisible by the divisor.

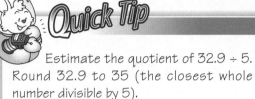

㊷ 49.82 ÷ 5 **Estimate** : ________ = ____

㊸ 53.84 ÷ 7 **Estimate** : ________ = ____

㊹ 46.23 ÷ 9 **Estimate** : ________ = ____

Quick Tip

Estimate the quotient of 32.9 ÷ 5.
Round 32.9 to 35 (the closest whole number divisible by 5).

35 ÷ 5 = 7

The quotient of 32.9 ÷ 5 is about 7.

Do the calculation mentally.

Examples

① 38.47 x 10 = 384.7
38.47 x 100 = 3847.0

When multiplied by 10 or 100, move the decimal point 1 or 2 places to the right.

② 38.4 ÷ 10 = 3.84
38.4 ÷ 100 = 0.384

When divided by 10 or 100, move the decimal point 1 or 2 places to the left.

③ 1.6 x 30
= 1.6 x 3 x 10
= 4.8 x 10
= 48

㊺ 9.83 x 100 = ________

㊻ 12.93 x 10 = ________

㊼ 45.2 ÷ 10 = ________

㊽ 12.84 ÷ 10 = ________

㊾ 91.23 x 10 = ________

㊿ 16.3 ÷ 100 = ________

(51) 0.8 x 100 = ________

(52) 0.8 ÷ 10 = ________

(53) 1.2 ÷ 10 = ________

(54) 0.3 x 40 = ________

(55) 2.4 x 30 = ________

(56) 100 x 9.91 = ________

(57) 2.4 x 20 = ________

(58) 3.17 x 20 = ________

(59) 1.2 x 400 = ________

(60) 5.5 x 40 = ________

(61) 3.09 x 50 = ________

(62) 0.54 x 800 = ________

In each problem, put a decimal point in the right place of the shaded number to get the given answer. Add zeros if necessary.

(63) 5 6 8 x 10 = 56.8

(64) 3 8 ÷ 10 = 0.38

(65) 2 1 x 100 = 210

(66) 1 2 3 x 10 = 123

(67) 7 2 x 10 = 7.2

(68) 5 2 0 ÷ 100 = 0.52

Kim and Karen go shopping. Help them solve the problems. Show your work.

⑥⑨ Kim pays for a blouse with a $100 bill. How much change does she get?

$ 29.95

_____ = _____

She gets $ _____ change.

⑦⓪ Kim also pays for a pair of sandals with three $20 bills. How much change does she get?

$ 52.99

⑦① How much does Kim pay altogether for the blouse and sandals?

⑦② Karen buys 3 computer games. How much does she pay altogether?

$ 12.75

⑦③ How much does each pair of socks cost?

10 pairs for $ 32.60

⑦④ They each order the same lunch. How much do they pay altogether?

$ 6.93

⑦⑤ Each sweater costs $42.50. Karen buys 4 sweaters. How much does she pay?

Buy 3 Get 1 Free

⑦⑥ They share the cost of a teddy bear for Jane. How much does each one pay?

$ 78.50

MIND BOGGLER

Kim and Karen buy a gift for Darren. Kim pays $10 more than Karen. How much does each pay?

Kim pays $ _____ and Karen pays $ _____ .

$ 46.40

4 More about Basic Operations

Example

$5 \times 7 \times 2 = 2 \times 7 \times 5$
$= 7 \times 2 \times 5$
$= 7 \times 10$
$= 70$

You can multiply the numbers in any order. The easiest way is to multiply the numbers with a product of 10, 100... first.

Do the following multiplication mentally.

① $2 \times 9 \times 5$ = _____

② $5 \times 12 \times 2$ = _____

③ $20 \times 3 \times 5$ = _____

④ $17 \times 5 \times 2$ = _____

⑤ $2 \times 392 \times 5$ = _____

⑥ $5 \times 137 \times 20$ = _____

Estimate each of the following products to the nearest hundred by rounding the factors to the nearest ten.

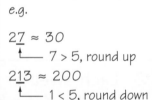

Quick Tip

When rounding a number, round up if the number to be considered is 5 or more; otherwise, round down,
e.g.

$2\underline{7} \approx 30$
⌐ 7 > 5, round up
$2\underline{1}3 \approx 200$
⌐ 1 < 5, round down

⑦ 36×72

Estimate : _____ x _____

= _____

⑧ 25×95

Estimate : _____ x _____

= _____

⑨ 61×39

Estimate : _____ x _____

= _____

⑩ 17×81

Estimate : _____ x _____

= _____

Estimate the answers by rounding the numbers, except the 1-digit numbers, to the nearest hundred.

⑪ $529 + 398 - 199$ **Estimate** : $\underline{500 + 400 - 200}$ = _____

⑫ $781 - 239 + 99$ **Estimate** : _____ = _____

⑬ $1523 - 398 - 721$ **Estimate** : _____ = _____

⑭ $301 - 99 + 215 + 39$ **Estimate** : _____ = _____

⑮ $2594 \div 2$ **Estimate** : _____ = _____

⑯ $3025 \div 6$ **Estimate** : _____ = _____

⑰ $1234 \div 4$ **Estimate** : _____ = _____

Solve the following multi-step problems. Show your work.

⑱ There are 4 rows of 6 desks and 2 rows of 5 desks
in a classroom. How many desks are there in all?

There are _____ desks in all.

⑲ In a concert hall, there are 50 rows with 35 seats in each row. All the seats
are filled and 32 people have to stand at the back. How many people are
there in all?

⑳ 69 students go on a field trip. 45 of them go by bus. The others go by van
with 6 passengers in each van. How many vans are needed?

㉑ There are 78 guests at Mrs. Wong's party. In the dining room, there are 5 oval
tables with 8 seats each and 7 round tables with 6 seats each. How many empty
seats are there?

㉒ Anna can swim 9 lengths of a pool in 5 minutes. How many lengths can she
swim in 30 minutes?

㉓ If the pool is 25 m long, how many metres does Anna swim in 30 minutes?

A medium-sized car uses 9 L of gas for 100 km of town driving and 7 L of gas for highway driving. Solve the problems by completing the tables.

㉔ How far can this car travel in town on 45 L of gas?

Distance travelled (km)	100	
Gas used (L)	9	45

It can travel _____ km.

㉕ How many L of gas are needed to travel 50 km in town?

Distance travelled (km)	100	50
Gas used (L)		

_____ L of gas are needed.

㉖ How many L of gas are needed for a 600-km highway journey?

Distance travelled (km)	100	600
Gas used (L)		

_____ L of gas are needed.

㉗ Gas costs 70¢ per litre. How much will a 600-km highway journey cost?

Gas used (L)	1	
Cost ($)		

It will cost $ _____ .

㉘ A new "Envirocar" uses only 4 L of gas for 100 km on the highway. How much can be saved on a 600-km journey as compared with a medium-sized car?

	Distance travelled (km)	Gas used (L)	Cost ($)
Envirocar	100	4	
	600		
Medium-sized car	600		

Amount saved: _____ = _____

㉙ The medium-sized car and the Envirocar start from Acton and complete a round trip as the diagram shows. Find the gas cost of each car.

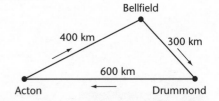

	Distance travelled (km)	Gas used (L)	Cost ($)
Medium-sized car			
Envirocar			

Pete, Paul and Sue are collecting baseball cards.
A pack of 20 cards costs $1.79. Estimate and
solve the two-step problems.

③⓪ Pete has 320 cards. Estimate the
total cost of the cards to the
nearest whole number. _____

③① Paul's cards cost him $17.90 in
all. How many cards does he
have? _____

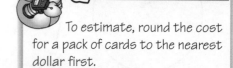
Quick Tip

To estimate, round the cost
for a pack of cards to the nearest
dollar first.

③② Sue has $10 to spend on cards.
How many packs can she buy? _____

③③ How much change does Sue get? _____

③④ How much more money must Sue save until she
can buy another pack? _____

③⑤ Mr. Wu takes Pete, Paul and Sue to a baseball game by train. Baseball tickets
cost $35 each. The train fare is $9 for an adult and $6 for a child. Estimate first
and then find the exact amount that Mr. Wu has to pay in all.

Estimate: _____ Exact amount: _____

③⑥ How much change does Mr. Wu get from two
$100 bills? _____

③⑦ Each bag of popcorn costs $4. What is the maximum
number of bags of popcorn that Mr. Wu can buy
with the change? _____

MIND BOGGLER

How many handshakes?

5 friends meet at the baseball game.
They each shake hands once with
their friends. How many handshakes
are there in all?

There are ___25___ handshakes in all.

5 Units of Measure

Use a ruler and a piece of string to find the circumference and diameter of each of the following circles in cm to the nearest tenth.

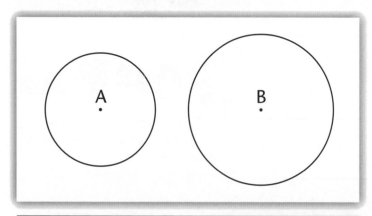

Circle	A	B
① Circumference (cm)		
② Diameter (cm)		

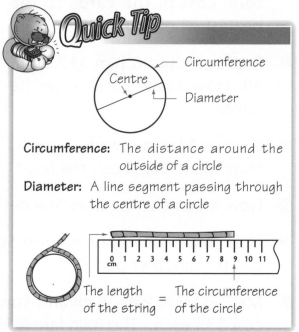

Quick Tip

Circumference

Centre

Diameter

Circumference: The distance around the outside of a circle

Diameter: A line segment passing through the centre of a circle

The length of the string = The circumference of the circle

Find these objects at home and measure their circumferences to the nearest cm using a string and a ruler.

③   ④    ⑤   ⑥

_____ cm   _____ cm   _____ cm   _____ cm

If the lamp post is 4 m tall, estimate the height of the other objects in the picture in metres.

⑦ Height of the fence = _____

⑧ Height of the tree = _____

⑨ Height of the building = _____

Ground

Complete the table.

	Date	Date in SI notation
⑩	November 29, 1943	
⑪	February 5, 2001	
⑫		2002 09 24
⑬		2003 03 20

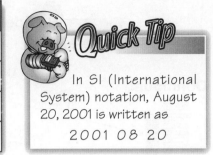

Quick Tip

In SI (International System) notation, August 20, 2001 is written as

2001 08 20

Calculate the number of days between the following dates.

⑭ From 2002 03 21 to 2002 05 01 _____ days

⑮ From 2002 12 20 to 2003 01 27 _____ days

Write the times or draw the clock hands to show the given times to the nearest minute.

⑯ _____

⑰ _____

⑱ 11:35

⑲ 2:28

Calculate the time intervals.

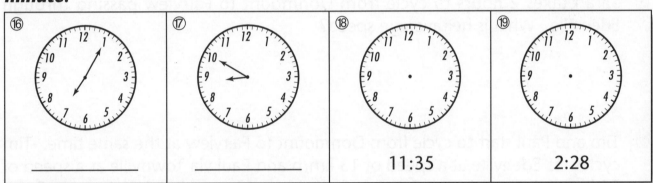

Examples

① From 7:30:20 a.m. to 9:00 a.m.

9:00 ⟶ 8:59:60
(1 h = 60 min)   − 7:30:20
(1 min = 60 s)   1:29:40

The time interval is 1 h 29 min 40 s.

② From 7:30 a.m. to 2:15 p.m.

12:00 noon ⟶ 11:60   4:30 (in the morning)
           − 7:30   + 2:15 (in the afternoon)
           4:30   6:45

The time interval is 6 h 45 min.

⑳ 9:12:05 a.m. to 9:46:23 a.m. _____

㉑ 3:07:26 p.m. to 3:12:09 p.m. _____

㉒ 8:15:34 a.m. to 11:23:12 a.m. _____

㉓ 6:30:00 a.m. to 7:55:00 p.m. _____

㉔ 11:10:20 a.m. to 12:13:10 p.m. _____

Use the diagram to solve the problems. Show your work.

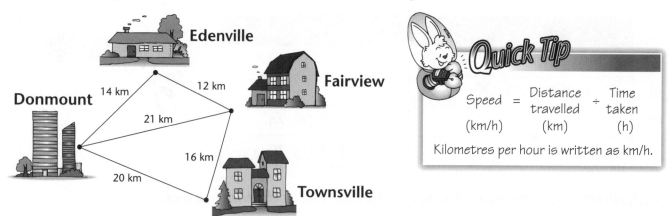

25 It takes Sam 1 hour to cycle from Edenville to Fairview. What is his speed?

His speed is _____ km/h.

26 Sarah takes 2 hours to cycle from Donmount to Fairview passing through Edenville. What is her average speed?

27 Tim and Paul start to cycle from Donmount to Fairview at the same time. Tim cycles via Edenville at a speed of 13 km/h and Paul via Townville at a speed of 12 km/h. Who arrives at Fairview first? How much earlier does he arrive?

28 a. A car travels at 40 km/h. Complete the table to show how far it can travel in the given times.

Time (h)	1	$\frac{1}{2}$	$\frac{1}{4}$	$\frac{3}{4}$	$1\frac{1}{2}$
Distance travelled (km)	40				

b. How long does it take to drive from Donmount to Townville directly? _____

c. How long does it take to drive back and forth 5 times between Fairview and Edenville? _____

**The distance around the track at Donville school
is 250 m. Solve the problems.**

29 Ron is training for the school track meet. He runs
around the track 8 times.

a. How many metres has he run?   _____

b. How many kilometres has he run? _____

Quick Tip

1 km = 1000 m
1 cm = 10 mm
1 m = 10 dm = 100 cm

30 Sarah records Ron's time. Write the times and
calculate how long Ron's run takes.

a. Starting time   _____

b. Finishing time   _____

c. Time taken in minutes _____

d. Time taken in hours   _____

Start	Finish

31 If Ron continued at the same speed, how many
km could he run in half an hour?   _____

32 At what speed in km/h does Ron run?   _____

33 Janice can jog around the same track 4 times in
10 minutes. Write how far she can cover

a. in 10 minutes (in metres).   _____

b. in 60 minutes (in metres).   _____

c. in 10 minutes (in kilometres).   _____

d. in 60 minutes (in kilometres).   _____

34 What is Janice's speed in km/h?   _____

MIND BOGGLER

How many times within 24 hours would the two hands of a
clock overlap?

Two clock hands would overlap ___24___ times within 24 hours.

Perimeter and Area

Use a ruler to measure the perimeter of each shape to the nearest cm.

① _____ cm

② _____ cm

Quick Tip

The perimeter of a shape is the distance around the outside of the shape.

③ _____ cm

④ _____ cm

⑤ _____ cm

Find the perimeters (P) of the following shapes.

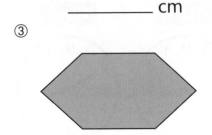

⑥ 2 cm 2 cm 1 cm 1 cm 3 cm 3 cm

P = _____

⑦ 6 m 4 m 7 m 4 m 6 m

P = _____

⑧ 13 dm 5 dm 12 dm

P = _____

⑨ 4 dm 2 dm 4 dm 5 dm 5 dm

P = _____

⑩ 8 cm 5 cm 5 cm 14 cm

P = _____

⑪ 4.5 m 4.5 m 4.5 m 4.5 m

P = _____

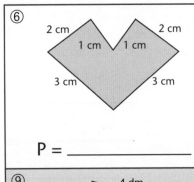
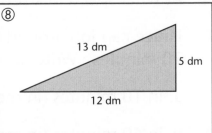
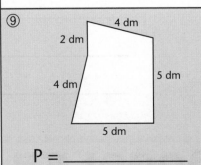
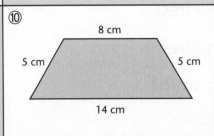
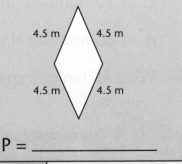

⑫ 6 mm 12 mm 3 mm 12 mm 6 mm

P = _____

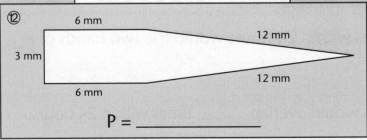

Count the squares to estimate the areas of the following irregular shapes to the nearest cm².

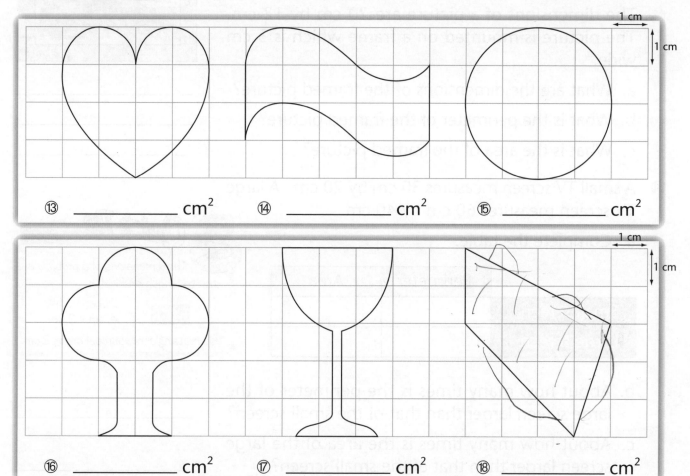

⑬ _____ cm²   ⑭ _____ cm²   ⑮ _____ cm²

⑯ _____ cm²   ⑰ _____ cm²   ⑱ _____ cm²

Calculate the perimeters (P) and areas (A) of the following shapes.

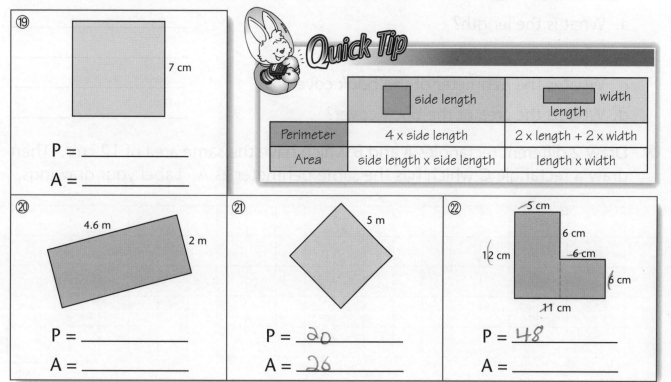

⑲ 7 cm

P = _____
A = _____

Quick Tip

	side length	width length
Perimeter	4 x side length	2 x length + 2 x width
Area	side length x side length	length x width

⑳ 4.6 m, 2 m

P = _____
A = _____

㉑ 5 m

P = 20
A = 26

㉒ 5 cm, 6 cm, 6 cm, 12 cm, 6 cm, 11 cm

P = 48
A = _____

Solve the problems.

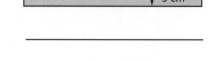

㉓ The dimensions of a picture are 20 cm by 12 cm. The picture is mounted on a frame which is 3 cm wide.

a. What are the dimensions of the framed picture? _____

b. What is the perimeter of the framed picture? _____

c. What is the area of the framed picture? _____

㉔ A small TV screen measures 30 cm by 20 cm. A large TV screen measures 60 cm by 40 cm.

a. Complete the table.

	Perimeter	Area
Small screen		
Large screen		

> **Quick Tip**
> The dimensions of a rectangle are its length and width.
> 4 cm
> 2 cm
> Dimensions : 4 cm x 2 cm
> This rectangle measures 4 cm by 2 cm.

b. About how many times is the perimeter of the large screen larger than that of the small screen? _____

c. About how many times is the area of the large screen larger than that of the small screen? _____

㉕ Measure the length and width of this book to the nearest cm.

a. What is the length? _____

b. What is the width? _____

c. What is the perimeter of the book cover? _____

d. What is the area of the book cover? _____

㉖ Draw 2 different rectangles A and B which have the same area of 12 cm². Then draw a rectangle C which has the same perimeter as A. Label your drawings.

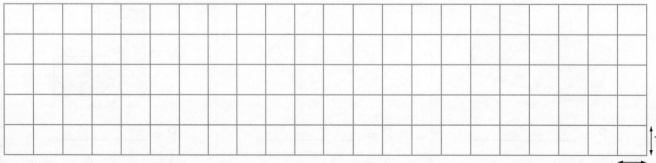

1 cm

1 cm

Katie is going to refurbish her bedroom. Look at the diagram and solve the problems.

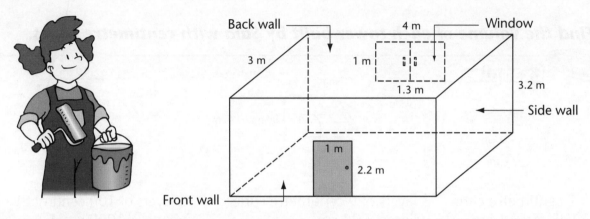

㉗ Katie wants to cover the whole floor with a carpet. What is the area of the carpet? _____

㉘ What is the area of the window? _____

㉙ What is the area of the door? _____

㉚ What is the perimeter of the floor? _____

㉛ New wood trim is put around the edge of the floor, except for the door. How much wood trim is needed? _____

㉜ What is the area of one side wall? _____

㉝ What is the area of the front wall including the door? _____

㉞ Katie paints her bedroom walls pink but not the door, window, floor or ceiling. What is the total area to be painted?

_____

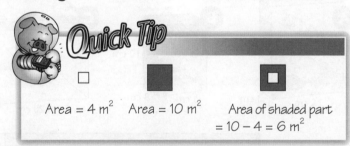

Quick Tip

Area = 4 m²   Area = 10 m²   Area of shaded part = 10 − 4 = 6 m²

MIND BOGGLER

How to divide?

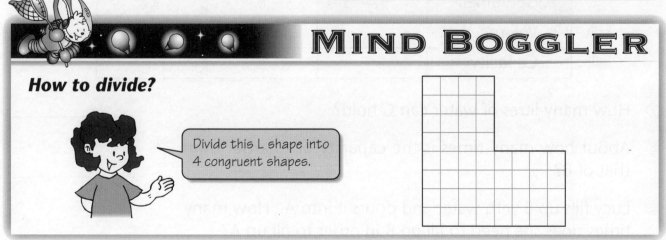

Divide this L shape into 4 congruent shapes.

7 Volume, Capacity and Mass

Find the volume of each tower built by Sam with centimetre cubes.

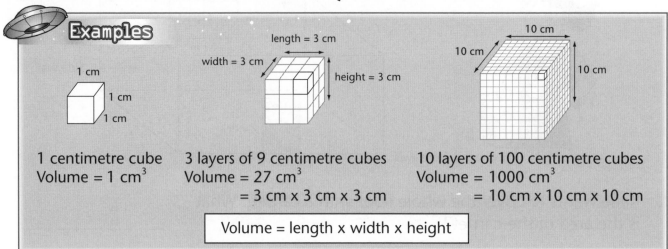

Examples

1 centimetre cube
Volume = 1 cm^3

3 layers of 9 centimetre cubes
Volume = 27 cm^3
= 3 cm x 3 cm x 3 cm

10 layers of 100 centimetre cubes
Volume = 1000 cm^3
= 10 cm x 10 cm x 10 cm

Volume = length x width x height

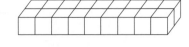
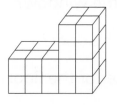
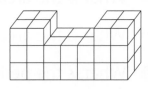

① _____ cm^3 ② _____ cm^3 ③ _____ cm^3 ④ _____ cm^3

Help Sam calculate the volume and capacity of each container. Then answer the questions.

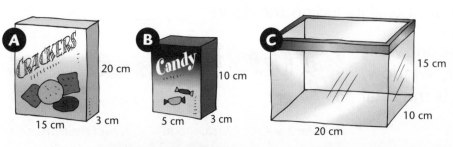

Quick Tip

Capacity (the greatest amount of liquid a container can hold) can be measured by the volume of the container.
1 millilitre = 1 cubic centimetre
1 mL = 1 cm^3
1 L = 1000 mL

Container	A	B	C
⑤ Volume			
⑥ Capacity			

⑦ How many litres of water can C hold? _____

⑧ About how many times is the capacity of C larger than that of B? _____

⑨ Lucy fills up B with water and pours it into A. How many times does she need to fill up B in order to fill up A? _____

30

Solve the problems.

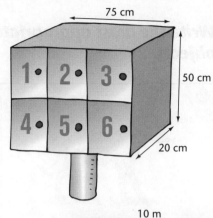

75 cm

50 cm

20 cm

⑩ A communal mailbox contains 6 identical mailboxes. What are the dimensions of each mailbox?

_____

⑪ What is the volume of each mailbox?

_____

10 m

2 m

2 m

⑫ What is the volume of the truck's container?

_____

⑬ Estimate the number of boxes, each measuring 0.5 m x 1 m x 1 m, that could be transported in this container.

_____

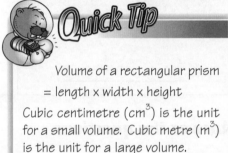

Quick Tip

Volume of a rectangular prism = length x width x height

Cubic centimetre (cm^3) is the unit for a small volume. Cubic metre (m^3) is the unit for a large volume.

Find the volume of each of the irregular objects by measuring the amount of liquid displaced by the object.

⑭

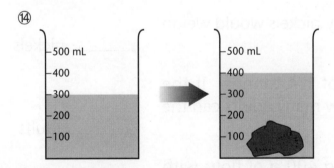

Amount of liquid displaced = _____ mL

Volume of the stone = _____ cm^3

⑮

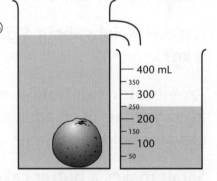

Volume of the orange

= _____ cm^3

⑯ A fish tank has a square base measuring 30 cm by 30 cm. When Sam puts a stone into the tank, the water level rises by 5 cm.

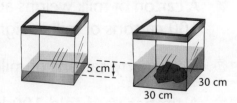

5 cm

30 cm

30 cm

Volume of water displaced = _____ x _____ x _____ = _____ cm^3

Volume of the stone = _____ cm^3

Write the most appropriate standard units to measure the mass of the following objects.

Quick Tip

Mass can be measured in milligram (mg), gram (g), kilogram (kg) or tonne (t).

1 t = 1000 kg
1 kg = 1000 g
1 g = 1000 mg

⑰ _____

⑱ _____

⑲ _____

⑳ _____

㉑ _____

Answer the questions.

㉒ Baby Jack weighed 3.2 kg at birth and gained 100 g per week. How much did he weigh at 12 weeks? _____ kg

㉓ A nickel weighs about 5 g. How many nickels would weigh 1 kg? _____ nickels

㉔ An elevator can hold a maximum of 1.4 tonnes. If the average mass of an adult is 70 kg, how many adults can the elevator hold each time? _____ adults

㉕ Sarah makes a butter cake by mixing 400 g of flour with 250 g of sugar. How much flour would she need for 1 kg of sugar? _____ kg

㉖ A carton of milk weighs about 2.5 kg. How many kg would 100 cartons of milk weigh? _____ kg

㉗ How many cartons of milk would weigh 1 t? _____ cartons

㉘ A timber-yard sold 100 kg of logs for $5.00. How much can the yard get from selling 30 t of logs? $ _____

㉙ How much can the yard get from selling 30 000 g of logs? $ _____

Sam is holding a birthday party. Help him solve the problems.

㉚ Find the volume of 3 gift boxes Sam received.

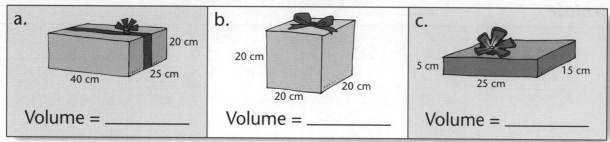

a.	b.	c.
20 cm, 40 cm, 25 cm	20 cm, 20 cm, 20 cm	5 cm, 25 cm, 15 cm
Volume = _____	Volume = _____	Volume = _____

㉛
12 cm   12 cm   4 cm   The dimensions of Sam's birthday cake are 12 cm x 12 cm x 4 cm. What is the volume of the cake?

_____

㉜ The cake is cut into 16 equal slices. What are the dimensions of each slice?

_____

㉝ What is the volume of each slice?

_____

㉞ The whole cake has a mass of 640 g. What is the mass of each slice?

_____

㉟ How many slices of cake would have a total mass of

a. 1 kg? _____   b. 1 t? _____

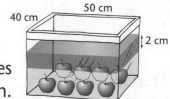

㊱ The children play the game "Bobbing for apples". 8 apples are dropped into the fish tank, and the water rises by 2 cm.

a. What is the total volume of the 8 apples?

_____

b. What is the average volume of each apple?

_____

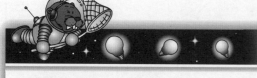

MIND BOGGLER

Which one is fake?

A jeweller has 8 gems, but one is fake and weighs less than the others. At least how many times does the jeweller need to weigh the gems with a balance in order to find out the fake one?

He needs to weigh at least _____ times.

Calculate.

①	②	③	④
5984 + 2079 – 3475	53 x 69	76 x 98	8⟌6296

Write the missing numbers in the equivalent fractions.

⑤ $\frac{15}{25} = \frac{}{5}$

⑥ $\frac{4}{9} = \frac{24}{}$

⑦ $\frac{28}{44} = \frac{7}{}$

Write the fractions as decimals.

⑧ $\frac{57}{100} =$ _____

⑨ $\frac{7}{10} + \frac{9}{100} =$ _____

⑩ $\frac{19}{50} =$ _____

Compare each pair of fractions. Put > or < in the circles.

⑪ $\frac{2}{3} \bigcirc \frac{5}{9}$

⑫ $\frac{3}{4} \bigcirc \frac{4}{5}$

⑬ $\frac{3}{8} \bigcirc \frac{1}{2}$

Find the answers.

⑭	⑮	⑯	⑰
5.98 + 7.23	7.16 – 2.97	6.23 x 8	8⟌6.32

Calculate mentally.

⑱ 15.93 x 100 = _____

⑲ 6.08 ÷ 10 = _____

⑳ 7.8 x 2 x 50 = _____

㉑ 3 x 5 x 20 = _____

㉒ 50 x 17 x 2 = _____

㉓ 32 x 4 x 25 = _____

㉔ 10 x 40 x 3 = _____

㉕ 4 x 27 x 25 = _____

㉖ 50 x 2 x 16 = _____

㉗ 4 x 15 x 20 = _____

34

Count the squares on the grid to estimate the areas of the following shapes to the nearest cm².

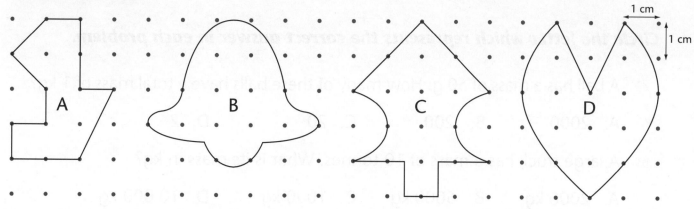

1 cm

1 cm

㉘ A = _____ cm² ㉙ B = _____ cm² ㉚ C = _____ cm² ㉛ D = _____ cm²

Calculate the perimeter (P) and area (A) of each of the following shapes.

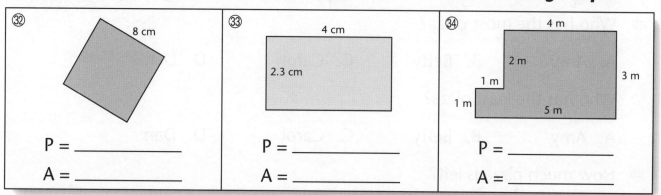

㉜ 8 cm

P = _____

A = _____

㉝ 4 cm

2.3 cm

P = _____

A = _____

㉞ 4 m

2 m

1 m

1 m

3 m

5 m

P = _____

A = _____

Calculate the volume (V) of each of the following objects.

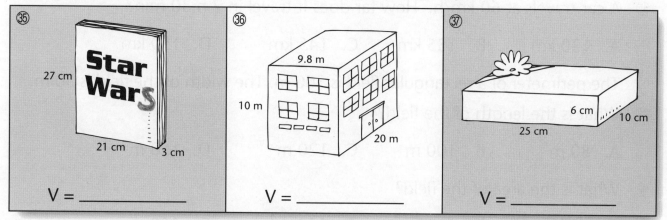

㉟ **Star Wars**

27 cm

21 cm

3 cm

V = _____

㊱ 9.8 m

10 m

20 m

V = _____

㊲ 6 cm

25 cm

10 cm

V = _____

Find the answers.

㊳ Fast Freddie runs 100 m in 14 seconds. If he starts at 11:58:50, at what time will he reach the finish line?

_____

㊴ John starts his 50-day diet on March 28. On which day will his diet end?

_____

Circle the letter which represents the correct answer in each problem.

④⓪ A ball has a mass of 50 g. How many of these balls have a total mass of 1 kg?

    A. 2000   B. 200   C. 20   D. 2

④① A large truck has a mass of 10 tonnes. What is its mass in kg?

    A. 2000 kg   B. 5000 kg   C. 1000 kg   D. 10 000 kg

4 friends share 2 pizzas. Amy has $\frac{1}{3}$ of a pizza, Betty has $\frac{1}{4}$, Carol has $\frac{2}{3}$, and Dan has $\frac{7}{12}$.

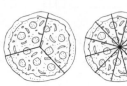

④② Who has the most pizza?

    A. Amy   B. Betty   C. Carol   D. Dan

④③ Who has the least pizza?

    A. Amy   B. Betty   C. Carol   D. Dan

④④ How much pizza is left?

    A. $\frac{1}{12}$ B. $\frac{1}{6}$ C. $\frac{1}{4}$ D. $\frac{1}{3}$

④⑤ A car travels at 60 km/h. How far does it travel in 2 h 30 min?

    A. 130 km   B. 135 km   C. 145 km   D. 150 km

The perimeter of a rectangular field is 300 m. The width of the field is 50 m.

④⑥ What is the length of the field?

    A. 80 m   B. 100 m   C. 120 m   D. 150 m

④⑦ What is the area of the field?

    A. 5000 m²   B. 5000 m   C. 350 m²   D. 350 m

④⑧ Which of the following is an equivalent fraction of $\frac{3}{5}$?

    A. $\frac{1}{3}$ B. $\frac{6}{10}$ C. $\frac{34}{54}$ D. $\frac{9}{25}$

④⑨ 12 min 13 s after 11:50:48 p.m. is _____ .

    A. 12:02:01   B. 12:03:01   C. 00:02:01   D. 00:03:01

Solve the problems. Show your work.

50 The aquarium is filled with water to a depth of 20 cm.

a. What is the volume of the water in cm³?

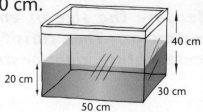

40 cm

20 cm

30 cm

50 cm

b. Some stones are put into the aquarium and the water level is now 25 cm high. What is the volume of the stones in cm³?

c. What is the capacity of the aquarium in L?

51 In the school hall, there are 17 rows with 18 chairs each and 3 rows with only 15 chairs each.

a. How many students can be seated in the hall ?

b. If 360 students attend an assembly in the hall, how many students have to stand?

c. There is 1 teacher for every 20 students in the hall. How many teachers are there in the hall?

d. The clock faces show the starting time and the finishing time of the assembly. How long does the assembly last?

8 Angles and 2-D Figures

Measure the size of each angle using a protractor. Then classify each angle as an acute, obtuse, right or straight angle.

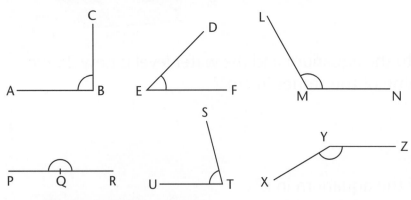

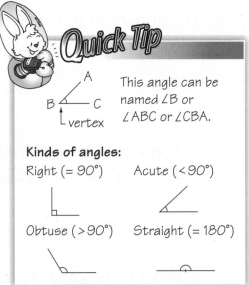
Angle	∠ABC	∠DEF	∠LMN	∠PQR	∠STU	∠XYZ
① Size in degrees						
② Kind of angle						

Draw the following angles using a protractor.

③ 68°	④ 135°	⑤ 90°

Complete the triangles. Then measure the angles and lengths.

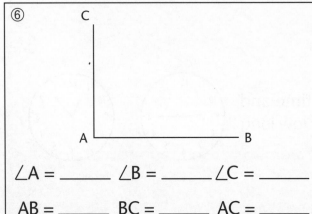

⑥

∠A = _____   ∠B = _____   ∠C = _____

AB = _____   BC = _____   AC = _____

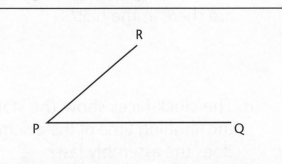

⑦

∠P = _____   ∠Q = _____

PR = _____   QR = _____

Classify ΔABC and ΔPQR drawn in ⑥ and ⑦.

Classification according to	Δ ABC	Δ PQR
⑧ Length of sides		
⑨ Size of angles		

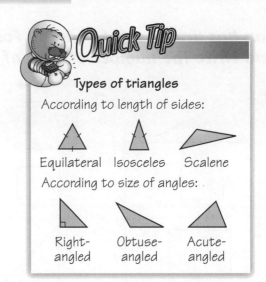

Quick Tip

Types of triangles

According to length of sides:

Equilateral   Isosceles   Scalene

According to size of angles:

Right-angled   Obtuse-angled   Acute-angled

Draw the triangles.

⑩ A right-angled isosceles triangle	⑪ An obtuse-angled scalene triangle	⑫ An acute-angled isosceles triangle

Look at the new logo designs for LR Inc. and answer the questions.

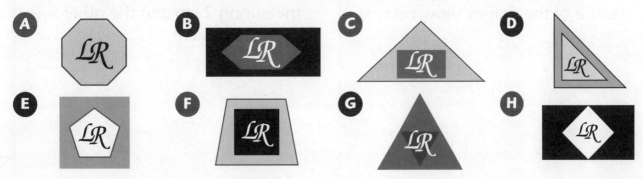

A   B   C   D

E   F   G   H

⑬ Which design is a trapezoid? _____

⑭ Which design contains a pentagon? _____

⑮ Which design is an octagon? _____

⑯ Which design contains a hexagon? _____

⑰ How many triangles are there altogether? _____

⑱ How many rectangles are there altogether? _____

⑲ How many quadrilaterals are there altogether? _____

Ron has drawn some shapes. For each shape draw all the lines of symmetry and write the number of lines of symmetry in the box.

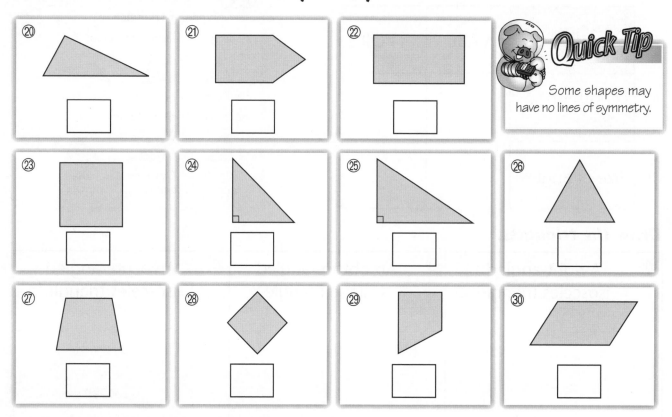

Quick Tip

Some shapes may have no lines of symmetry.

Follow the instructions to construct 2-D figures.

③① Construct a figure with only one vertical line of symmetry using at least 2 of the shapes shown above.

③② Construct 2 different right-angled triangles, both with one side measuring 2 cm and the other side measuring 3 cm.

Name the following 2-D figures.

③③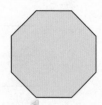

③④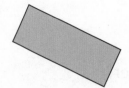

③⑤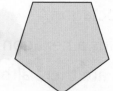

③⑥

_____   _____   _____   _____

For each of the figures on the left, look for its congruent and similar figures on the right. Colour the congruent figure red and the similar figure yellow.

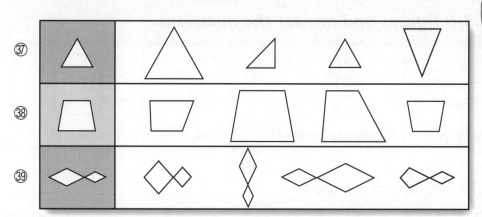

Congruent figures
- figures with the same shape and size

Similar figures
- figures with the same shape but different sizes

Draw a congruent and a similar figure for each of the following shapes.

Shape	Congruent figure	Similar figure
㊵		
㊶		
㊷		

MIND BOGGLER

Think and count.

How many squares are there altogether?

There are ____14____ squares.

9 3-D Figures

Look at the following 3-D figures and answer the questions.

Cube	Rectangular prism	Rectangular pyramid	Cone	Cylinder

① What is the shape of each face of a cube? _____

② How many faces does a cube have? _____

③ What is the shape of each face of a rectangular prism? _____

④ How many faces does a rectangular pyramid have? _____

    Write the names of its faces. _____

⑤ Which solids have a curved surface? _____

⑥ What is the shape of the base of those solids which have a curved surface? _____

⑦ How many vertices does a rectangular prism have? _____

⑧ How many edges does a cube have? _____

⑨ How many polyhedra are there? _____

⑩ What are they?

_____

Quick Tip

A polyhedron is a 3-D solid that has only polygonal surfaces. Polyhedra is the plural of polyhedron.

Which of the following nets make a cube? Put a check mark ✔ in the box.

⑪

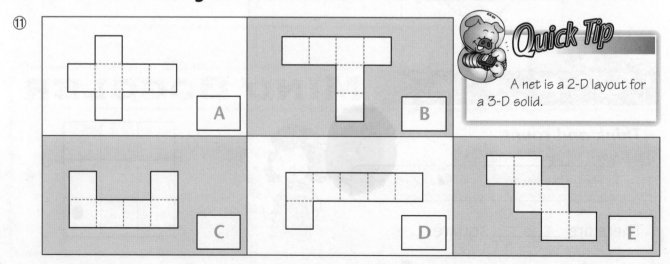

Quick Tip

A net is a 2-D layout for a 3-D solid.

A   B   C   D   E

Look at the following pyramids. Complete the table and the statements.

⑫ Number of vertices				
⑬ Number of edges				
⑭ Number of faces				
⑮ Number of triangular faces				
⑯ Shape of base				

⑰ The number of _____ and the number of _____ are the same.

⑱ The number of _____ equals the number of sides of the base.

⑲ The number of _____ is twice the number of sides of the base.

⑳ The number of vertices is _____ more than the number of sides of the base.

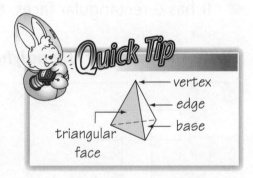

Quick Tip

vertex
edge
base
triangular face

Which of the following nets make a pyramid? Put a check mark ✔ in the box.

㉑

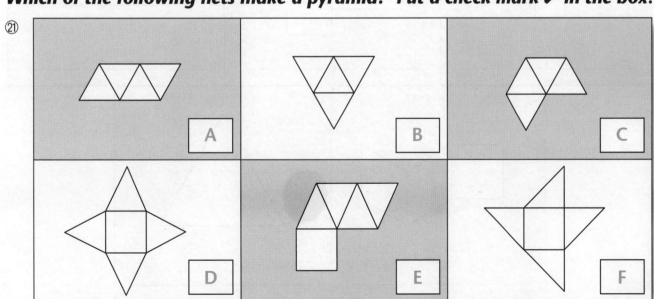

A

B

C

D

E

F

Read the clues and name the solids. The following figures may help you guess the answers.

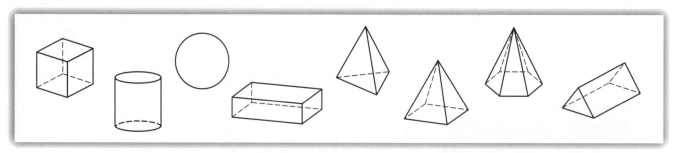

㉒ It has 4 faces, 4 vertices and 6 edges.   _____

㉓ It has 6 square faces, 8 vertices and 12 edges.   _____

㉔ It has no flat surfaces.   _____

㉕ It has only 2 flat surfaces.   _____

㉖ It has 7 faces, 7 vertices and 12 edges.   _____

㉗ It has 5 faces, 6 vertices and 9 edges.   _____

㉘ It has 6 rectangular faces, 8 vertices and 12 edges.   _____

Write the name of the polyhedron which can be made from each net below.

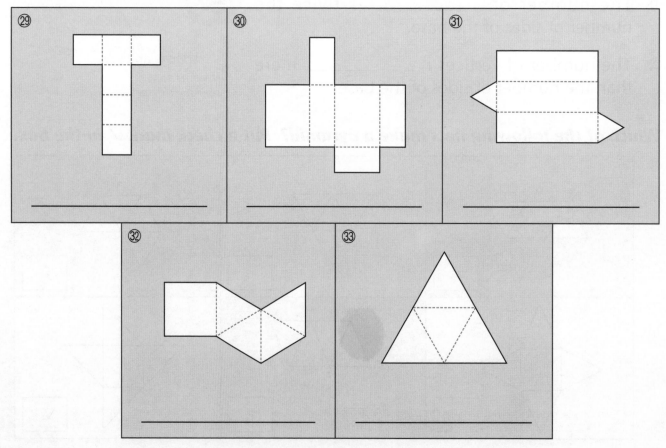

Write the name of each solid.

Top view	▲	⊙	■	▽	▬
Side view	▲	△	■	▯	▬
Name of the solid	㉞	㉟	㊱	㊲	㊳

Lali uses cubes to build different structures. Draw what he sees if he looks at the structures from the top, front or side.

	Whole structure	Top view	Front view	Side view
㊴	top view ← / → side view / front view	□□		
㊵				
㊶				
㊷				

MIND BOGGLER

How to do it?

I can use 3 sticks to form a triangle.

Can you use 9 sticks to form 7 triangles?

10 Coordinates and Transformations

In Newton the avenues and streets are laid out in a grid pattern. Plot each of the following sites on the grid and label each with the representing letter and the ordered pair. Then answer the questions.

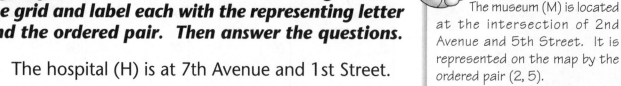

Quick Tip

The museum (M) is located at the intersection of 2nd Avenue and 5th Street. It is represented on the map by the ordered pair (2, 5).

① The hospital (H) is at 7th Avenue and 1st Street.

② The school (S) is at 4th Avenue and 8th Street.

③ The park (P) is at 6th Avenue and 8th Street.

④ The library (L) is at 5th Avenue and 3rd Street.

⑤ The food court (F) is in the mall at 6th Avenue and 2nd Street.

⑥ The doctor's office (D) is at 2nd Avenue and 1st Street.

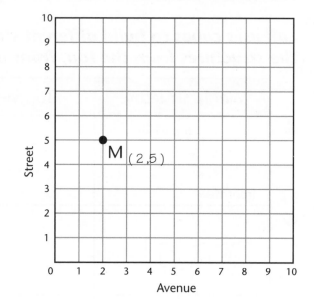

⑦ The video store (V) on 1st Street is the same distance from the library and the hospital. What is the ordered pair of the video store?

_____

⑧ The museum is the same distance from the library and the swimming pool (W). The swimming pool is the same distance from the school and the park. What is the ordered pair of the swimming pool?

_____

⑨ The library is of equal distance from two different places. What are they?

_____

⑩ What is 3 units down and 4 units right from the museum? _____

⑪ What is 5 units up and 1 unit right from the library? _____

⑫ Is the museum closer to the doctor's office or the school?

_____

⑬ Is the video store closer to the library or the doctor's office?

_____

Help Tia rotate the letters of her name as instructed. Draw the images.

⑭ $\frac{1}{4}$ turn counterclockwise

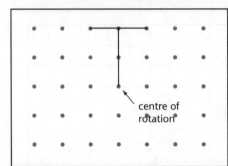

⑮ $\frac{1}{4}$ turn clockwise

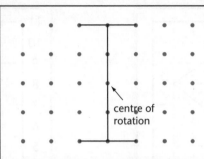

⑯ $\frac{1}{2}$ turn clockwise

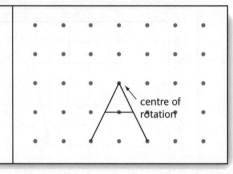

Help Harmit Ali reflect her initials in different lines of reflection. Draw the images.

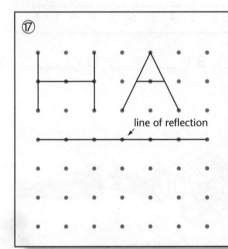

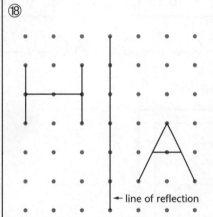

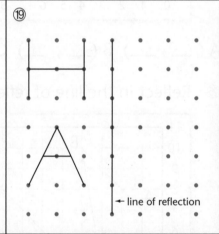

Help Indira Lal translate her initials as described. Draw the images.

⑳ 4 blocks right and 3 blocks down

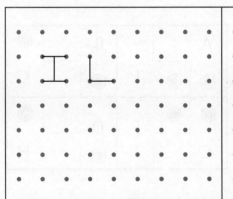

㉑ 2 blocks up and 4 blocks left

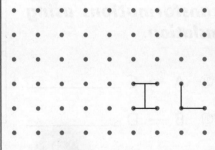

㉒ 2 blocks down and 3 blocks right

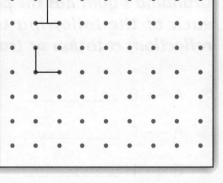

Draw the transformed images as instructed and write the ordered pairs of the vertices of the images.

㉓ Translate 4 units down and 5 units left.

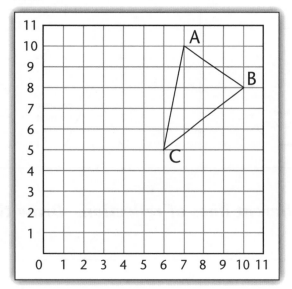

A (___ , ___) B (___ , ___) C (___ , ___)

㉔ Make a $\frac{1}{2}$ turn clockwise about the centre of rotation.

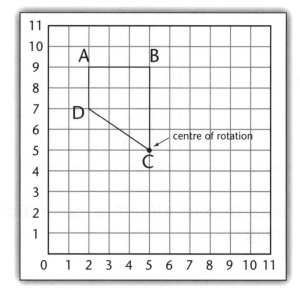

A (___ , ___) B (___ , ___) D (___ , ___)

㉕ Reflect in the line of reflection.

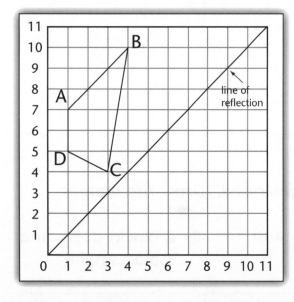

A (___ , ___)

B (___ , ___)

C (___ , ___)

D (___ , ___)

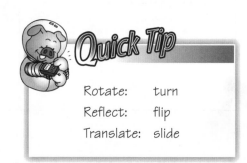

Rotate: turn
Reflect: flip
Translate: slide

Grandma's quilt has the pattern shown. Describe each of the following transformations using reflection, rotation or translation.

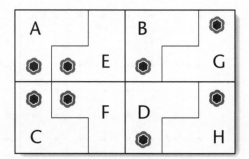

㉖ A → B _____

㉗ A → C _____

㉘ A → F _____

㉙ B → D _____

㉚ C → H _____

㉛ E → F _____

㉜ A → D _____

Grandma's pattern can tile a plane. Put a check mark ✔ in the box if the shape can form a tiling pattern.

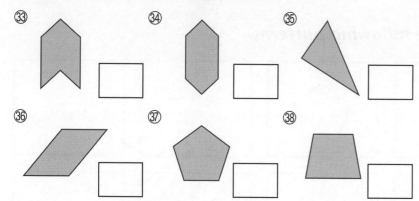

㉝　　㉞　　㉟

㊱　　㊲　　㊳

Look at the triangles drawn on the grid and answer the questions. Write the letters only.

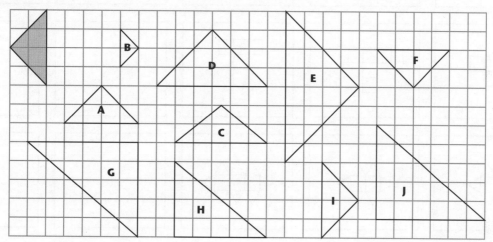

㊴　Which triangles are congruent to the shaded triangle?　　_____

㊵　Which triangles are similar to the shaded triangle?　　_____

MIND BOGGLER

Complete a parallelogram.

① On the grid provided, plot the following points.

A (4,7)　　B (2,5)　　C (4,4)

② Write the coordinates of the 4th point so that the four points form a parallelogram. There are 3 possible answers. Plot all the possible 4th points.

The 4th point can be _____ .

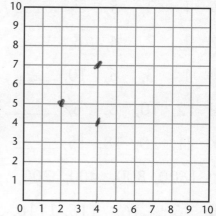

11 Patterns

Fill in the empty boxes in the following patterns.

① 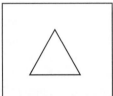 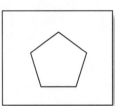   

②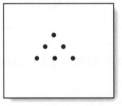

③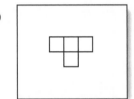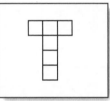

④

⑤

Look for the patterns and then add the next 3 numbers for each pattern.

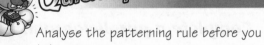

Quick Tip

Analyse the patterning rule before you extend the pattern,

e.g. 10, 20, 30, ...

Each number in this pattern is 10 more than the previous number. This number pattern with 3 more terms is :

10, 20, 30, *40*, *50*, *60*

⑥ 1,   3,   5,   7, _____ , _____ , _____

⑦ 1,   2,   4,   8, _____ , _____ , _____

⑧ 1,   3,   6,   10, _____ , _____ , _____

⑨ 12, 10, 8,   6, _____ , _____ , _____

⑩ 21, 20, 18, 15, _____ , _____ , _____

⑪ 1600, 800, 400, 200, _____ , _____ , _____

⑫ 6,   16, 116, 1116, _____ , _____ , _____

Describe in words the patterns of the numbers in the following number sequences.

⑬ 6, 11, 16, 21, ... _____

⑭ 5, 10, 20, 40, ... _____

⑮ 62, 55, 48, 41, ... _____

⑯ 480, 240, 120, 60, ... _____

Saiko and Suniko made up some code and so they can send secret messages to each other. Look for the letter patterns and complete the tables below to find the codes by continuing the patterns. Help them decode the messages.

⑰
A	B	D	G			
1	2	3	4	5	6	7

⑱
C	E	H	L		
8	9	10	11	12	13

⑲
F	I	M		
14	15	16	17	18

⑳
J	N	S	
19	20	21	22

㉑ If O,T,Z and U are represented by 23, 24, 25 and 26 respectively, decode this message sent by Saiko to Suniko.

11, 9, 24, 21   4, 23   24, 23   1   16, 23, 7, 15, 9   24, 23, 20, 15, 4, 10, 24

_____

㉒ Suniko sends a reply to Saiko. Decode her message.

13, 10, 15, 8, 10   16, 23, 7, 15, 9   3, 23   22, 23, 26   13, 1, 10, 24

24, 23   21, 9, 9 ?

_____

Identify changes in terms of two variables and extend the patterns. Fill in the missing numbers.

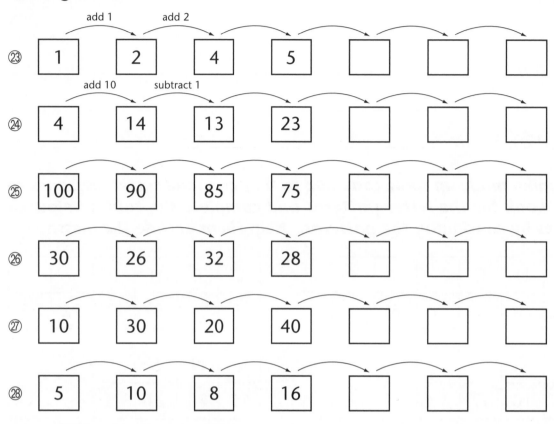

㉓ add 1   add 2

| 1 | 2 | 4 | 5 | | | |

㉔ add 10   subtract 1

| 4 | 14 | 13 | 23 | | | |

㉕

| 100 | 90 | 85 | 75 | | | |

㉖

| 30 | 26 | 32 | 28 | | | |

㉗

| 10 | 30 | 20 | 40 | | | |

㉘

| 5 | 10 | 8 | 16 | | | |

For each group of numbers, write the rule that you can use to obtain the 2nd number from the 1st number. Then follow the rule to write two more pairs of numbers for each group.

㉙
1st number	2	3	5		
2nd number	6	9	15		

Rule : _____
_____

㉚
1st number	12	18	24		
2nd number	6	9	12		

Rule : _____
_____

㉛
1st number	1	4	7		
2nd number	1	7	13		

Rule : _____
_____

㉜
1st number	4	6	10		
2nd number	3	4	6		

Rule : _____
_____

Look at the pattern that grows as you add triangles with toothpicks. Draw two more diagrams, complete the table and answer the questions.

㉝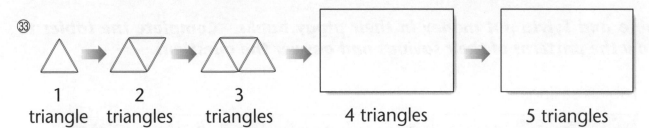

| 1 triangle | 2 triangles | 3 triangles | 4 triangles | 5 triangles |

㉞

Number of triangles	1	2	3	4	5	6	7	8
Number of toothpicks	3	5	7					

㉟ How many toothpicks are used to make a pattern with 10 triangles? _____ toothpicks

㊱ How many triangles can be formed using 27 toothpicks? _____ triangles

㊲ What is the pattern of the number of toothpicks shown in ㉞?

_____

㊳ Describe a rule that relates the number of triangles to the number of toothpicks.

_____

_____

MIND BOGGLER

Calculate the distances.

Annie the ant is crawling along a 1-m log. She crawls $\frac{1}{2}$ of the distance on the 1st day, and $\frac{1}{2}$ of the remaining distance on the 2nd day.

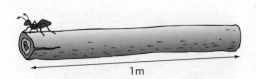

1m

① How far does she crawl on the 4th day? _____ cm

② What distance remains for Annie to crawl after the 4th day? _____ cm

③ By following this crawling pattern, is it possible for Annie the ant to reach the other end of the 1-m log? _____

53

12 Using Patterns and Simple Equations

Fabio and Sylvia put money in their piggy banks. Complete the tables to show the patterns of their savings and answer the questions.

① Fabio's savings

Day	1	2	3	4	5	6	7	8
Savings (¢)	20	30	40					

② On which day will Fabio put one dollar into his piggy bank?   Day _____

③ How much will Fabio put into the piggy bank on Day 12? $ _____

④ Sylvia's savings

Day	1	2	3	4	5	6	7	8
Savings (¢)	55	60	65					

⑤ On which day will Sylvia put one dollar into her piggy bank?   Day _____

⑥ How much will Sylvia put into the piggy bank on Day 12? $ _____

Ms. Ling's science class is growing bean plants from seeds. Complete the table to show the pattern of growing and answer the questions.

Day	3	4	5	6	7	8
⑦ Number of seeds sprouted	2	4	6			
⑧ Height of the tallest plant (cm)	0.5	1.0	1.5			

⑨ How many seeds will have sprouted by the 10th day?   _____ seeds

⑩ How long will it take till all 20 seeds have sprouted?   _____ days

⑪ When will the tallest plant reach 3.5 cm?   Day _____

⑫ What is the height of the tallest plant on Day 10?   _____ cm

54

Ms. White's Grade 5 class has collected food items for the local food bank for 9 weeks. Help the children solve the problems.

⑬ Complete the table by continuing the pattern.

Week	1	2	3	4	5	6	7	8	9
Number of items collected	2	4	8	10	14	16	20	22	

⑭ Describe in words the pattern shown in the table.

_____

⑮ How many items has the class collected over the 9 weeks? _____

Mrs. Wong put $250 in a special account when her son, Rob, was born. The account doubles in value every 5 years. Help them solve the problems.

⑯ Complete the table to find out how much money Rob will have when he is 20 years old.

Age	at birth	5	10	15	20
Amount ($)	250				

⑰ Rob decides to buy a used car for $1000 on his 20th birthday and invests the rest of the money in an account which doubles in value for every 6 years. Complete the table below to find out how much money Rob will have when he is 38 years old.

Age	20			
Amount ($)				

⑱ Which account is a better investment, the one which doubles every 6 years or the one which doubles every 5 years? Explain.

_____

_____

_____

The table below shows how the mass of Gerry the Gerbil increases as he gets older. Solve the problems.

⑲ Complete the table by continuing the pattern.

Age (Week)	at birth	1	2	3	4	5	6
Mass (g)	20	30	35	45	50		

⑳ Describe in words the pattern shown in the table.

_____

㉑ If this pattern continues, when will he have a mass of 90 g? _____

㉒ Pam says that as Gerry's age doubles, his mass also doubles. Is that true? Explain.

_____

Ali, Ben, Shari and Sam are training for athletic meets. Help them solve the problems.

㉓ Ali is a sprinter. He runs the same distance each day. On the 1st day, it takes him 5 min 36 s. On the 2nd day, it takes him 5 min 30 s, and on the 3rd day, it takes him 5 min 24 s. Assume that this trend continues,

   a. how long will his run take on the 5th day? _____

   b. when will his run take 5 minutes? _____

㉔ Ben is a long distance runner. He runs many times around the track. The 1st lap takes 5 min, the 2nd 5 min 20 s, and the 3rd 5 min 40 s.

   a. How long will his 6th lap take? _____

   b. Which lap will take him 7 min? _____

㉕ Shari is a long jumper. She jumps 2.5 m on Day 1, 2.55 m on Day 2, and 2.6 m on Day 3. If this trend continues,

   a. how far will she jump on Day 5? _____

   b. when will she jump 3 m? _____

㉖ Sam is a high jumper. He jumps 1.42 m in the 1st attempt, 1.43 m in the 2nd attempt, and 1.44 m in the 3rd attempt. If this trend continues,

   a. how high will he jump in the 5th attempt? _____

   b. in which attempt will he jump 1.5 m? _____

Fill in the missing numbers in the following equations.

Quick Tip

Use the guess-and-test method to find the missing terms or factors in simple equations.

㉗ 17 + ____ = 26 ㉘ 39 – ____ = 11

㉙ 2 x ____ = 20 ㉚ 50 ÷ ____ = 25

㉛ 93 + ____ = 209 ㉜ 15 x ____ = 450

㉝ 720 ÷ ____ = 36 ㉞ 150 ÷ ____ = 3 ㉟ 7 x ____ = 630

㊱ ____ ÷ 2 = 17 ㊲ 502 – ____ = 410 ㊳ 10 x ____ = 5

㊴ 52 x ____ = 5.2 ㊵ 12 x ____ = 0.12 ㊶ 12 ÷ ____ = 1.2

㊷ 1.2 ÷ ____ = 0.6 ㊸ 10 x ____ = 12 ㊹ 15 x ____ = 1.5

㊺ 5.9 + ____ = 7.3 ㊻ 12.7 – ____ = 6.8 ㊼ ____ – 3.4 = 7.8

㊽ 1.2 x ____ = 6.0 ㊾ 3.7 x ____ = 370 ㊿ 49 ÷ ____ = 4.9

(51) ____ ÷ 5 = 1.2 (52) ____ ÷ 8 = 12 (53) ____ x 3 = 36

Check ✔ the right equations.

(54) 6 more than a number y is 15.

A 6 – y = 15 B 6 + y = 15 C y – 6 = 15

(55) 4 less than a number b is 12.

A b + 4 = 12 B 4 – b = 12 C b – 4 = 12

(56) 3 times a number p is 27.

A 3 x p = 27 B p ÷ 3 = 27 C 3 ÷ p = 27

MIND BOGGLER

What is Rachel's number?

I think of a number. I double it and add 10. Then I divide the answer by 2 and get a final answer of 35.

Rachel's number is ________ .

13 Data and Graphs

The teachers at a local school were asked what types of cars they drive. The results of the survey are shown in the pictograph below.

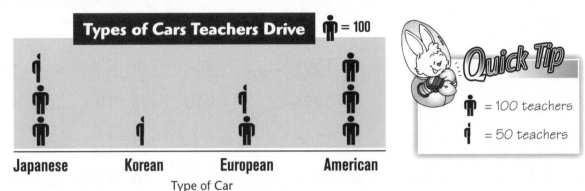

Types of Cars Teachers Drive = 100

Japanese   Korean   European   American

Type of Car

Quick Tip

 = 100 teachers

 = 50 teachers

① Which type of car is the most popular? _____

② Which type of car is the next popular? _____

③ Which type of car is the least popular? _____

④ How many teachers drive European cars? _____

⑤ How many teachers drive Japanese or Korean cars? _____

⑥ How many teachers do not drive American cars? _____

⑦ How many more teachers drive Japanese cars than Korean cars? _____

⑧ How many teachers were surveyed altogether? _____

⑨ What type of car makes up $\frac{1}{3}$ of all the cars? _____

⑩ The school also uses a circle graph to show the results of the survey. Label each sector of the circle with the type of car represented.

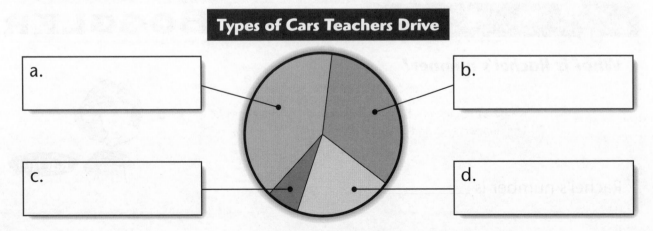

Types of Cars Teachers Drive

a.

b.

c.

d.

A group of children surveyed among themselves their favourite ball games on TV. The results of the survey are shown in the graph below.

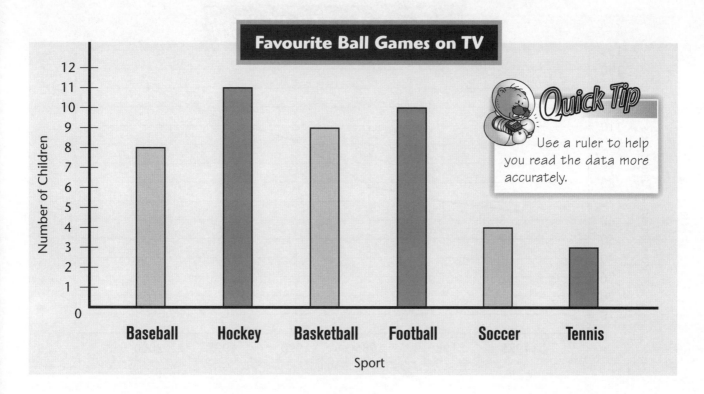

Favourite Ball Games on TV

Quick Tip

Use a ruler to help you read the data more accurately.

⑪ Which is the most popular ball game? _____

⑫ Which is the least popular ball game? _____

⑬ How many children chose soccer? _____

⑭ How many children chose football or basketball? _____

⑮ How many more children chose basketball than tennis? _____

⑯ How many fewer children chose soccer than football? _____

⑰ How many types of ball games were chosen by more than 8 children? _____

⑱ How many children did not choose hockey or soccer? _____

⑲ How many children were surveyed altogether? _____

⑳ What fraction of the children surveyed chose football? _____

㉑ 2 girls chose baseball. What fraction of the children who chose baseball are girls? _____

㉒ What type of graph is used to show the results of this survey? _____

The line graph below shows how the population of Bellfield grew between 1975 and 2000. Use the graph to answer the questions.

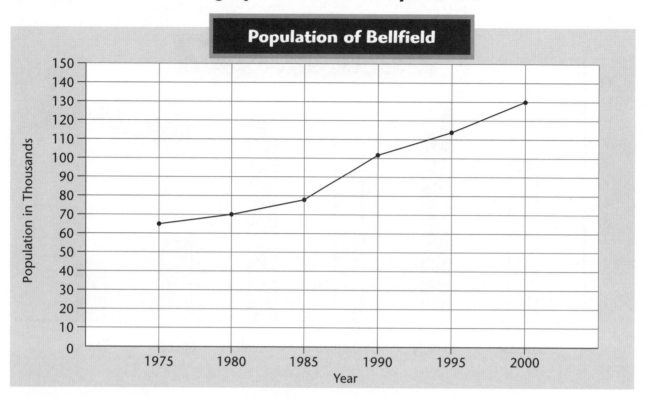

23 What was the population in 1975?   _____

24 What was the population in 2000?   _____

25 In which year did the population reach 100 000?   _____

26 What was the increase in population between 1980 and 1985?   _____

27 What was the increase in population between 1980 and 2000?   _____

28 During which period did the population increase the least?   _____

29 During which period did the population increase the most?   _____

30 If the trend continues, what will be the population in Bellfield in 2005? Explain.

_____

_____

_____

31 Which is better for showing population growth, a line graph or a bar graph? Explain.

_____

Example

Josh wrote 9 quizzes. Here are his results (out of 10):

2 5 9 7 8 6 7 5 5

What is his mean score?

Mean: $\dfrac{2+5+9+7+8+6+7+5+5}{9} = 6$ ← Add all the results. Then divide the total by the number of quizzes to get the mean score.

What is the mode of his scores?

The mode is 5. ← 5 occurs most among the 9 scores.

Mr. Smith conducted a survey in his Grade 5 class. Here are the results from 5 of the students. Help Mr. Smith solve the problems.

	Ali	Steve	Sam	Fabio	Sylvia
Number of pets in family	2	0	1	1	3
Number of children in family	3	2	4	2	1
Distance in km from home to school	5	8	2	7	5

㉜ Find the means. Write your answers correct to 1 decimal place.

Pets in the family _____

Children in the family _____

Distance in km from home to school _____

㉝ Find the modes.

Pets in the family _____

Children in the family _____

Distance in km from home to school _____

㉞ How many students have more pets than the mean? _____ students

㉟ Sam received a Labrador for his birthday. What are the mean and the mode of the number of pets in the family of these 5 students now?

Mean _____ Mode _____

MIND BOGGLER

What is the 5th number?

7	9	8	2	?

I choose 5 numbers. The mean of the numbers is 6.

The 5th number is _____ .

14 Probability

Example

Hannah has 3 shirts – red, white and yellow, and 2 skirts – blue and grey. Her different possible outfits can be shown by using a "tree diagram".

Shirt	Skirt	Outfit
red (R)	blue (B) –	RB
	grey (G) –	RG
white (W)	blue (B) –	WB
	grey (G) –	WG
yellow (Y)	blue (B) –	YB
	grey (G) –	YG

There are 6 possible outfits.

The probability that Hannah will choose a yellow shirt is $\frac{2}{6}$ ($\frac{1}{3}$ or 1 out of 3).

The probability that Hannah will choose a red shirt and a blue skirt is $\frac{1}{6}$ (1 out of 6).

Help Cindy find out the possible choices of poppy seed or sesame seed bagel that may have the filling of tuna (T), egg (E), or cheese (C).

① Complete the tree diagram to show her choices for lunch.

Bagel	Filling	Combination
Poppy seed (P)		
Sesame seed (S)		

② How many possible combinations are there for the lunch? _____

③ What is the probability that she will have a sesame seed bagel? _____

④ What is the probability that she will have tuna on her bagel? _____

⑤ What is the probability that she will have a sesame seed bagel with tuna? _____

Draw lines to join each of the following events to the probability associated with it.

Quick Tip

Probability can be written as fractions with the total possible outcomes as the denominator and the number of outcomes of a particular event as the numerator. The more probable the event, the larger the fraction is.

Event		Probability
⑥ Snow falls in Montreal in January. •		• $\frac{1}{10}$
⑦ Snow falls in Florida in March. •		• $\frac{9}{10}$
⑧ Snow falls in Toronto in March. •		• $\frac{1}{100}$

Stephen spins the spinner shown. Help him solve the problems.

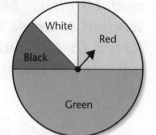

⑨ What colour is the spinner most likely to land on?

_____

⑩ Which colours is the spinner equally likely to land on?

_____

⑪ What is the probability that the spinner will land on red?   _____

⑫ What is the probability that the spinner will land on green?   _____

⑬ What is the probability that the spinner will land on green or red?

_____

⑭ If Stephen spins the spinner 100 times, how many times is it likely to land on red or green?

_____

Sarah rolls two dice and adds the numbers that come up. Use her results to solve the problems.

⑮ Complete the table to show all the possible sums.

+	1	2	3	4	5	6
1						
2						
3						
4						
5						
6						

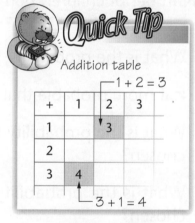

Addition table

1 + 2 = 3

+	1	2	3
1		3	
2			
3	4		

3 + 1 = 4

⑯ How many possible sums are there?   _____

⑰ How many different sums are possible?   _____

⑱ Which sum is most likely to come up? What is the probability to get this sum?   _____ ; _____

⑲ Which sums are least likely to come up? What is the probability to get each sum?   _____ ; _____

⑳ Which sum is as likely to get as 9?   _____

In Mr. Keller's Grade 5 class, there are 14 boys and 10 girls. Mr. Keller wants to choose a student to erase the blackboard. Refer to the table below and answer the questions.

$a + 5 = 8$
$a = 3$

Quick Tip
Don't forget to write fractions in lowest terms in your answers.

	Boys	Girls	Total no. of children
Number of children	14	10	24
Number of children with fair hair	4	8	12
Number of children with dark hair	10	2	12
Number of children born in Canada	12	6	18
Number of children born outside Canada	2	4	6

㉑ What is the probability that a girl will be chosen? _____

㉒ Is it more probable that Mr. Keller will choose a boy or a girl? _____

㉓ What is the probability that a student born in Canada will be chosen? _____

㉔ What is the probability that a girl born in Canada will be chosen? _____

㉕ What is the probability that a boy with fair hair will be chosen? _____

㉖ Is it less probable for Mr. Keller to choose a girl with fair hair than one with dark hair? _____

㉗ Mr. Keller wants to choose a girl to erase the blackboard. What is the probability that a girl with fair hair will be chosen? _____

㉘ On Monday, 1 girl and 2 boys were absent. What was the probability that Mr. Keller would choose a girl? _____

㉙ 3 new students, 1 boy and 2 girls, are added to Mr. Keller's class. They have recently arrived in Canada. What is the probability now that a boy born outside Canada will be chosen? _____

Riverview School is going to have its annual barbecue. The weather forecast says that there is a 1 out of 4 chance of rain on the day of the barbecue. The circle graphs below show the food, drinks and snacks prepared by the school. Refer to the graphs and answer the questions.

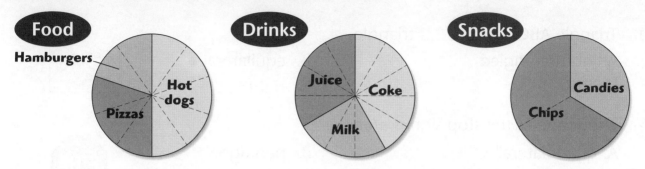

③⓪ What is the probability that a student will get a hamburger? _____

③① What is the probability that a student will get a coke? _____

③② What is the probability that a student will get chips? _____

③③ What is the probability that a student will get juice or milk? _____

③④ What is the probability that it will not rain on the day of the barbecue? _____

③⑤ What is the probability that a student will get a sandwich? _____

③⑥ Is it more likely for a student to get a pizza than a hamburger? _____

③⑦ Is it more likely for a student to get a bag of candies than chips? _____

③⑧ Is it more likely for a student to get a pizza than a hot dog? _____

MIND BOGGLER

In a single throw of a cube numbered 1 to 6, what is the probability of getting the numbers below?

① An even number _____

② A number greater than 6 _____

③ Any of the numbers from 1 to 6 _____

Quick Tip

When an event is impossible, its probability to happen is 0. When an event is certain to happen, its probability to happen is 1. The sum of the probabilities that all the possible events will happen is 1.

Final Test

Circle the letter which represents the correct answer in each problem.

① Triangle ABC is a/an ___D___ triangle.

   A. obtuse-angled   B. equilateral

   C. isosceles   D. right

② The shape of the stop sign is a/an ___C___ .

   A. quadrilateral   B. pentagon

   C. hexagon   D. octagon

③ Two triangles are similar if they

   A. have the same shape and size.

   B. have the same shape but different sizes.

   C. are both scalene triangles.

   D. are both right triangles.

④ The capital letter H has ___B___ lines of symmetry.

   A. 0   B. 1   C. 2   D. 3

⑤ A is a/an ___C___ angle.

   A. acute   B. obtuse

   C. reflex   D. right

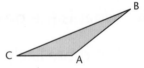

⑥ The net on the right is for a ___ .

   A. square pyramid   B. triangular pyramid

   C. cube   D. rectangular pyramid

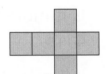

⑦ A solid with only 4 triangular faces is a ___ .

   A. tetrahedron   B. cone   C. pyramid   D. prism

⑧ The coordinates of point A are ___ .

   A. (0,4)   B. (3,0)

   C. (0,3)   D. (4,0)

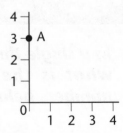

⑨ The coordinates of the image of point A after rotating through a quarter turn clockwise about (0,0) are ___ .

   A. (0,4)   B. (3,0)   C. (0,3)   D. (4,0)

⑩ A bag contains 5 blue marbles and 25 green marbles. The probability of picking a blue marble is ___ .

   A. $\dfrac{1}{5}$ B. $\dfrac{1}{6}$ C. $\dfrac{1}{3}$ D. $\dfrac{4}{5}$

⑪ The transformation which maps A onto B is _____ .

   A. Reflection   B. Rotation

   C. Translation   D. None of these

⑫ The transformation which maps A onto C is _____ .

   A. Reflection   B. Rotation

   C. Translation   D. None of these

⑬ The transformation which maps A onto E is _____ .

   A. Reflection   B. Rotation

   C. Translation   D. None of these

The tiling pattern for questions ⑪ – ⑭.

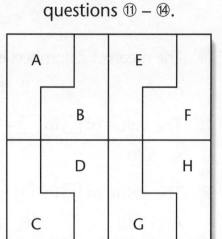

⑭ The transformation which maps B onto G is _____ .

   A. Reflection   B. Rotation

   C. Translation   D. None of these

⑮ The fraction of time in a day that Sam spends sleeping is _____ .

   A. $\dfrac{1}{3}$ B. $\dfrac{1}{4}$

   C. $\dfrac{1}{5}$ D. $\dfrac{1}{6}$

Sam's Daily Activities

(pie chart: Sleep, School, Relax, Eat)

⑯ Sam spends $\dfrac{1}{6}$ of the day _____ .

   A. sleeping   B. eating   C. relaxing   D. in school

⑰ The perimeter of the square is _____ .

   A. 52 cm   B. 52 cm^2

   C. 169 cm   D. 169 cm^2

13 cm
13 cm

⑱ The area of the square is _____ .

   A. 52 cm   B. 52 cm^2 C. 169 cm   D. 169 cm^2

⑲ The next 3 numbers in the pattern 4, 5, 7, 8, 10, ... are _____ .

   A. 11, 12, 13,   B. 11, 13, 14   C. 10, 11, 12   D. 10, 12, 13

⑳ The value of ☐ in 5 x ☐ = 7.05 is _____ .

   A. 2.05   B. 1.5   C. 35.25   D. 1.41

㉑ The mean of 2 numbers is 12. One of the numbers is 5. The other number is _____ .

   A. 7   B. 8.5   C. 19   D. 17

㉒ The value of ▢ in ▢ ÷ 100 = 5.2 is _____ .

   A. 520   B. 52   C. 0.52   D. 0.052

㉓ The value of ▢ in ▢ x 0.1=1.73 is _____ .

   A. 1730   B. 173   C. 17.3   D. 0.173

㉔ What is the 8th number in the pattern 1,2,3,5,8,...?

   A. 23   B. 15   C. 17   D. 34

㉕ 1 slice of cold meat has a mass of 40 g. How many slices of meat have a mass of 1 kg?

   A. 2.5   B. 25   C. 5   D. 50

㉖ Avi started his run around the track at 3:58:40 and finished at 4:02:15. How long was his run?

   A. 3 min 35 s   B. 4 min 25 s   C. 3 min 25 s   D. 4 min 35 s

㉗ The area of the shaded parallelogram is _____ square units.

   A. 5   B. 6

   C. 5.5   D. 6.5

㉘ The decimal 0.85 expressed as a fraction in lowest terms is _____ .

   A. $\frac{17}{20}$ B. $\frac{4}{5}$ C. $\frac{8.5}{10}$ D. $\frac{85}{100}$

㉙ The improper fraction $\frac{25}{4}$ expressed as a decimal is _____ .

   A. 2.13   B. 25.25   C. 6.25   D. 4.25

㉚ According to the weather forecast for today, the probability of rain is $\frac{1}{4}$, the probability of cloud is $\frac{1}{3}$, the probability of sun is $\frac{1}{5}$, and the probability of a thunderstorm is $\frac{1}{8}$. It is most likely that it will be _____ today.

   A. rainy   B. sunny   C. cloudy   D. stormy

Answer the questions. Show all your work.

㉛ In a hall there are 200 people. There are 15 rows of seats and each row has 13 seats. How many people are standing if all the seats are occupied?

㉜ Briana buys exercise books for her school. Each book costs $1.29.
   a. How many books can she get for $10?

   b. How much change does she get?

㉝ What is the remainder when 5982 is divided by 7? Check your answer.

㉞ A rock is put into the water as shown. Calculate the approximate volume of the rock in cm³.

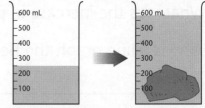

㉟ Tim earns $10.50 per hour. He works 9 hours a day, 5 days a week.
   a. How much does he earn per week?

   b. Last Sunday he was paid $78.75 for 5 hours of extra work. How much was his hourly wage on Sunday?

   c. How much did he earn last week?

The table shows the population of Greensville from 1960 to 2000. Use the data to make a line graph and answer the questions.

㊱

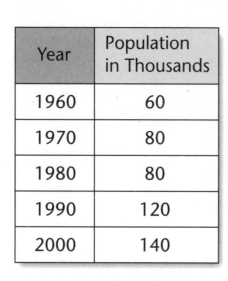

Year	Population in Thousands
1960	60
1970	80
1980	80
1990	120
2000	140

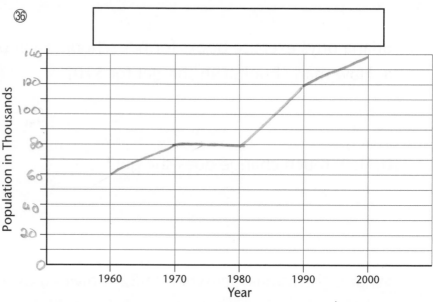

㊲ During which period was the increase in population the fastest? _____

㊳ In which year did the population reach 80 000? _____

㊴ What was the increase in population between 1960 and 2000? _____

㊵ Why is a line graph the best way to represent these data?

_____

This bar graph shows the colours of the cars in a parking lot. Use the graph to answer the questions. Write all fractions in lowest terms.

㊶ Read the graph and complete the table.

Colour	Number of Cars
Black	9
White	2
Green	4
Blue	5
Beige	6
Red	3

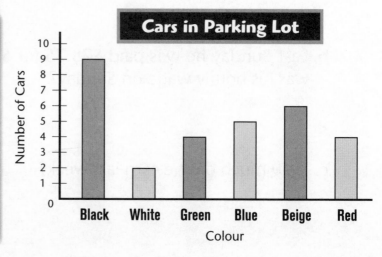

㊷ How many cars are there in the parking lot? ________

㊸ What fraction of the cars are beige? ________

㊹ What is the probability to find a blue car in the parking lot? ________

㊺ What is the probability that a car in the parking lot is red or green? ________

㊻ What is the probability that a car in the parking lot is not black? ________

A police officer is monitoring speeding on a suburban road. He records the following speeds of 6 cars in km/h: 50, 40, 45, 50, 84, 55.

㊼ What is the mean (average) speed of these 6 cars? ________ km/h

㊽ What is the mode of these speeds? ________ km/h

㊾ What is the mean speed of the remaining 5 cars after the fastest one is stopped by the police? ________ km/h

㊿ Has the mode changed after that? ________

(51) How long does it take to travel 25 km for a car going at 50 km/h? ________ min

(52) How far can a car travel in $1\frac{1}{2}$ h at an average speed of 45 km/h? ________ km

Look at the different rates offered by an Internet service provider. Answer the questions.

Package A	:	Unlimited use	\$39.99 per month
Package B	:	Up to 2 h per day	\$27.99 per month
Package C	:	Up to 1 h per day	\$14.99 per month

(53) Discuss how you would decide which is the best deal for you.

____

____

____

(54) The Browns use the Internet for $\frac{1}{2}$ h per day in June. Estimate how much Package C costs them per hour. ________

Dave and Dan each have a good collection of sports cards. The pictographs below show their collections.

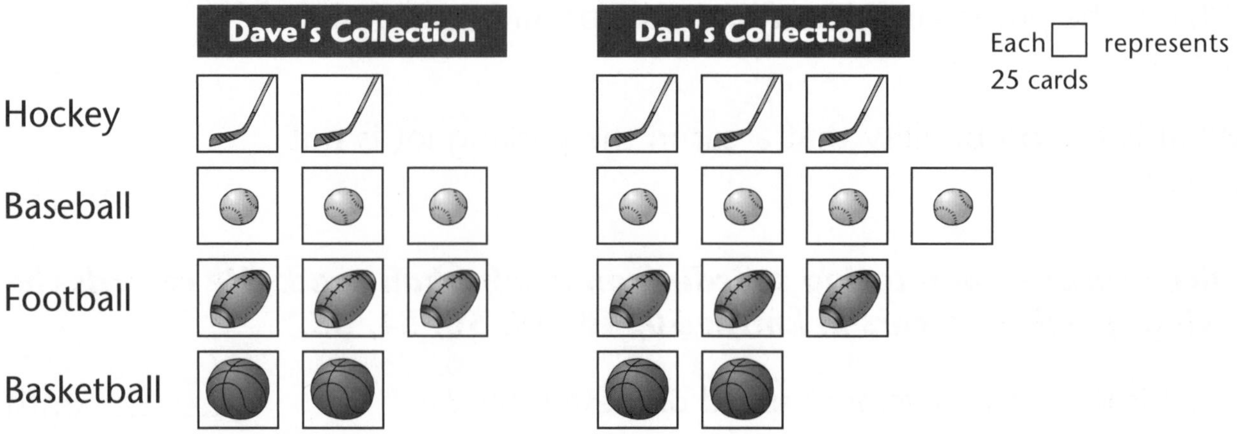

Dave's Collection	Dan's Collection	Each ☐ represents 25 cards

Hockey

Baseball

Football

Basketball

(55) How many cards has Dave collected? _____ cards

(56) How many cards has Dan collected? _____ cards

(57) What fraction of Dave's cards are hockey or baseball cards? _____

(58) What fraction of Dan's cards are basketball cards? _____

(59) How many football cards have they collected altogether? _____ cards

㊸ What fraction of their combined card collection are football cards? _____

� How many more baseball cards has Dan collected than Dave? _____ cards

(62) If their goal is to collect 1000 cards altogether, how many more cards must they collect? _____ cards

㊶ If the average cost of the cards is 5 for $1, what is the total value of their combined card collection? _____

The circle graphs below represent their card collections. Write the names of the sports to label the sectors of each circle.

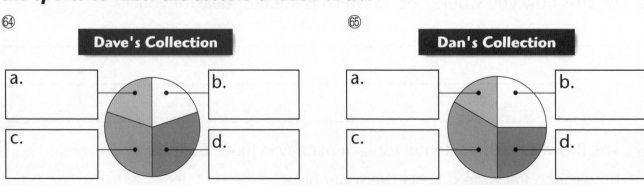

(64) Dave's Collection
a. b. c. d.

(65) Dan's Collection
a. b. c. d.

Review

1. 4282	2. 1944
3. 6720	4. 75
5. 3558	6. 3641
7. 216	8. 2884
9. 8000	10. 900

11. 40 ; 50 ; 60 ; 70 ; 80 ; 90 ; 100
12. 12 ; 15 ; 18 ; 21 ; 24 ; 27 ; 30
13. 36 ; 45 ; 54 ; 63 ; 72 ; 81 ; 90
14. 28 ; 35 ; 42 ; 49 ; 56 ; 63 ; 70
15. 60 ; 75 ; 90 ; 105 ; 120 ; 135 ; 150

16. 42	17. 24
18. 50	19. 54
20. 56	21. 72
22. 63	23. 80
24. 120	25. 90
26. 7	27. 5
28. 72	29. 98
30. 24	31. 123
32. 48	33. 38
34. 8	35. 8
36. 4	37. 8
38. 6	39. 15
40. 13	41. 4
42. 30	43. 20
44. 19	45. 16
46. 138	47. 6.0
48. 4.2	49. 6.5
50. 3.6	51. 11.6
52. 32.5	53. 24.8
54. 57.1	55. 281.7
56. 158.1	57. 33.4
58. 31.2	59. 52.1
60. 89.1	61. Steve
62. Sue	63. No

64. Steve, Paul, Stan, Sue

65. $\frac{9}{10}$	66. $\frac{4}{100}$
67. 0.25	68. 0.4
69. 0.3	70. 0.37
71. 1.02	72. 1.04
73. 1.05	74. 1.08
75. $1\frac{4}{8}$	76. $\frac{5}{8}$
77. $\frac{3}{8}$	78. 0.30
79. 50	80. 48.25
81. 6.75	82. 3.75
83. Reflection	84. Rotation
85. Translation	86. Reflection
87. 12 ; 9	88. 14 ; 10
89. 10 ; 6	

1   Operations with Whole Numbers

1. 8690	2. 7369
3. 902	4. 4214
5. 2288	6. 2355

7.
```
    54
  x 27
  ----
   378
  1080
  ----
  1458
```
8.
```
    38
  x 49
  ----
   342
  1520
  ----
  1862
```
9.
```
    17
  x 65
  ----
    85
  1020
  ----
  1105
```
10.
```
      742
  9 ) 6678
      63
      --
      37
      36
      --
       18
       18
```
11.
```
      92
  6 ) 559
      54
      --
      19
      18
      --
       1
```
12.
```
      702
  7 ) 4914
      49
      --
       14
       14
```

742 x 9 = 6678   92 x 6 + 1 = 559   702 x 7 = 4914

13. 1	14. 2
15. 0	16. 7
17. 8	18. 3
19. 4	20. 5
21. WELL DONE	22. ✔
23. ✔	24. 34
25. ✔	26. 20
27. ✔	28. ✔
29. ✔	30. 1
31. 20	32. 50
33. ✔	34. 4025
35. 1417	36. 980
37. 2265	38. 780
39. 81	40. 235
41. 1218	42. 3344
43. 120	44. 210
45. 4854	46. 8
47. 187	48. 29
49. 72	

50.

2	3	5	1	8	7
5	1	2	1	8	4
7	2	3	1	1	8
2	9	8	2	2	5
0	7	1	0	1	4
3	3	4	4	0	8

51. 16   52. 16
53. Time taken : 12 x 90 = 1080 ; 1080
54. Time taken : 15 x 75 = 1125
    He takes 1125 seconds to swim 15 lengths.
55. Difference : 1125 – 1080 = 45
    The difference between their times is 45 seconds.
56. Average number of swimmers : 1848 ÷ 7 = 264
    The average number of swimmers per day was 264.

Mind Boggler

40 ; 48

2   Fractions

1. 2	2. 2	3. 2	4. 14
5. 5	6. 1		
7. E	8. F	9. B	10. C
11. D	12. A		

13.
```
(1/3)  [▓ | | ]
(1/4)  [▓ | | | ]
```
14.
```
(1/2)  [▓ | ]
(2/5)  [▓ | | | ]
```

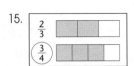

15.

$\frac{2}{3}$			

$\frac{3}{4}$			

16. T   17. T   18. F   19. T

20. F   21. T   22. F   23. T

24. F   25. F   26. F   27. T

28. $\frac{11}{4} > \frac{5}{2} > 2\frac{1}{5}$ 29. $\frac{7}{4} > \frac{6}{4} > \frac{7}{8}$

30. $3\frac{1}{3} > \frac{13}{4} > 3\frac{1}{6}$ 31. $\frac{13}{3} > \frac{4}{3} > \frac{3}{4}$

32. $\frac{3}{5}$; $\frac{17}{20}$; $\frac{27}{50}$; $\frac{9}{25}$; $\frac{3}{4}$; $\frac{19}{5}$ or $3\frac{4}{5}$; $\frac{3}{2}$ or $1\frac{1}{2}$

33. 0.6 ; 0.85 ; 0.54 ; 0.36 ; 0.75 ; 3.8 ; 1.5

34a. $\frac{1}{2}$; $\frac{1}{4}$; $\frac{3}{4}$ b. $\frac{1}{4} < \frac{1}{2} < \frac{3}{4}$

35a. $4\frac{1}{2}$ b. $1\frac{1}{2}$ c. $2\frac{1}{4}$

36a. 12   b. 5   c. $\frac{7}{10}$

  d. No.

    $30 \div 4 = 7R2$; 30 is not divisible by 4.

37a. Having snacks   b. Playing in the garden

38. (Suggested answers) $\frac{1}{4}$; $\frac{3}{12}$

39. $\frac{1}{3}$

40. $\frac{4}{16} = \frac{1}{4}$ 41. 0.18

42a. 0.3   b. 0.5   c. 0.2

Mind Boggler

    Jane

3   Decimals

1. 7.51   2. 9.00   3. 4.06   4. 7.52

5. 2.88   6. 2.38   7. 21.21   8. 20.52

9. 46.89   10. 49.07   11. 39.37   12. 41.46

13. 38.68   14. 33.73

15. $\frac{7}{100}$ 16. $\frac{9}{100}$; $\frac{49}{100}$ 17. 70 ; 7

18. $\frac{7}{10}$; $\frac{79}{100}$ 19. $\frac{65}{100}$ 20. $\frac{34}{100}$

21. $\frac{4}{10}$; $\frac{5}{100}$

22. 27.2   23. 18.5   24. 181.35   25. 27.12

26. 121.87   27. 5.58   28. 192.72   29. 37.5

30. ✔   31. ✗   32. ✗   33. ✗

34. ✔   35. ✗

36.
```
     7.3
7 ) 5 1.1
    4 9
    ─────
      2 1
      2 1
```

37.
```
      6.2 9
4 ) 2 5.1 6
    2 4
    ─────
      1 1
        8
      ─────
        3 6
        3 6
```

38.
```
      3.9 8
5 ) 1 9.9 0
    1 5
    ─────
      4 9
      4 5
      ─────
        4 0
        4 0
```

39. 12.31   40. 8.85   41. 6.75

42. $50 \div 5$; 10   43. $56 \div 7$; 8   44. $45 \div 9$; 5

45. 983   46. 129.3   47. 4.52   48. 1.284

49. 912.3   50. 0.163   51. 80   52. 0.08

53. 0.12   54. 12   55. 72   56. 991

57. 48   58. 63.4   59. 480   60. 220

61. 154.5   62. 432   63. 5.68   64. 3.8

65. 2.1   66. 12.3   67. 0.72   68. 52.0

69. $100 - 29.95 = 70.05$; 70.05

70. $20 \times 3 - 52.99 = 7.01$

    She gets $7.01 change.

71. $29.95 + 52.99 = 82.94$

    Kim pays $82.94 altogether.

72. $12.75 \times 3 = 38.25$

    She pays $38.25 altogether.

73. $32.60 \div 10 = 3.26$

    Each pair costs $3.26.

74. $6.93 \times 2 = 13.86$

    They pay $13.86 altogether.

75. $42.5 \times 3 = 127.50$

    She pays $127.50.

76. $78.5 \div 2 = 39.25$

    Each pays $39.25.

Mind Boggler

    $28.2 ; $18.2

4   More about Basic Operations

1. 90   2. 120

3. 300   4. 170

5. 3920   6. 13 700

7. 40 ; 70 ; 2800   8. 30 ; 100 ; 3000

9. 60 ; 40 ; 2400   10. 20 ; 80 ; 1600

11. 700   12. $800 - 200 + 100$; 700

13. $1500 - 400 - 700$; 400   14. $300 - 100 + 200 + 0$; 400

15. $2600 \div 2$; 1300   16. $3000 \div 6$; 500

17. $1200 \div 4$; 300

18. Number of desks : $4 \times 6 + 2 \times 5 = 24 + 10 = 34$

    34

19. Total number of seats : $50 \times 35 = 1750$

    Number of people in the hall : $1750 + 32 = 1782$

    There are 1782 people in all.

20. Number of students going by van : $69 - 45 = 24$

    Number of vans needed : $24 \div 6 = 4$

    4 vans are needed.

21. Total number of seats : $5 \times 8 + 7 \times 6 = 40 + 42 = 82$

    Number of empty seats : $82 - 78 = 4$

    There are 4 empty seats.

22. Number of lengths Anna swims in 30 minutes : $30 \div 5 \times 9 = 54$

    She can swim 54 lengths in 30 minutes.

23. Distance Anna swims in 30 minutes : $25 \times 54 = 1350$

    Anna swims 1350 metres in 30 minutes.

24. 500 ; 500   25. 9 ; 4.5 ; 4.5

26. 7 ; 42 ; 42   27. 42 ; 0.70 ; 29.40 ; 29.40

28. 2.80 ;   29. 1300 ; 91 ; 63.70 ;

    24 ; 16.80 ;   1300 ; 52 ; 36.40

    42 ; 29.40 ;

    $29.40 - 16.80$; $12.60

30. $32.00   31. 200 cards

32. 5 packs   33. $1.05

34. $0.74   35. Exact amount : $167

36. $33   37. 8 bags

Mind Boggler

    10

5 Units of Measure

1. 4.7 ; 6.3
2. 3.0 ; 4.0

3.-6. (Suggested answers)

3. 20.9
4. 36.4
5. 23.5
6. 23.5
7. 3 m
8. 7 m
9. 8 m
10. 1943 11 29
11. 2001 02 5
12. September 24, 2002
13. March 20, 2003
14. 40
15. 37
16. 7 : 05
17. 8 : 50

18.

19.

20. 34 min 18 s
21. 4 min 43 s
22. 3 h 7 min 38 s
23. 13 h 25 min
24. 1 h 2 min 50 s
25. Speed : 12 ÷ 1 = 12 ; 12
26. Distance travelled by Sarah : 14 + 12 = 26
    Speed : 26 ÷ 2 = 13
    Her average speed is 13 km/h.
27. Distance travelled by Tim : 14 +12 = 26

Distance travelled by Tim	13 km	26 km
Time	1 h	2 h

Distance travelled by Paul : 20 + 16 = 36

Distance travelled by Paul	12 km	36 km
Time	1 h	3 h

Time difference : 3 – 2 =1
Tim arrives at Fairview first. He arrives 1 h earlier.

28a. 20 ; 10 ; 30 ; 60
b. $\frac{1}{2}$h

c. 3 h
29a. 2000 m
b. 2 km
30a. 3;35
b. 3:50
c. 15 min
d. $\frac{1}{4}$ h or 0.25 h

31. 4 km
32. 8 km/h
33a. 1000 m
b. 6000 m
c. 1 km
d. 6 km
34. 6 km/h

Mind Boggler

22 ;

Within 12 hours the minute hand moves 12 complete turns while the hour hand moves only 1 complete turn, so the two hands overlap 11 times. They overlap 22 times in 24 hours.

6 Perimeter and Area

1. 12
2. 12
3. 10
4. 13
5. 10
6. 12 cm
7. 27 m
8. 30 dm
9. 20 dm
10. 32 cm
11. 18 m
12. 39 mm
13. 12
14. 10
15. 12
16. 12
17. 6
18. 10

19. 28 cm ; 49 cm²
20. 13.2 m ; 9.2 m²
21. 20 m ; 25 m²
22. 46 cm ; 96 cm²
23a. 26 cm by 18 cm
b. 88 cm
c. 468 cm²
24a. Small screen : 100 cm ; 600 cm²
    Large screen : 200 cm ; 2400 cm²
b. 2 times
c. 4 times
25a. 29 cm
b. 21cm
c. 100 cm
d. 609 cm²
26. (Suggested drawings)

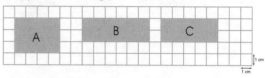

A : area = 12 cm² ; perimeter = 14 cm
B : area = 12 cm²
C : perimeter = 14 cm
27. 12 m²
28. 1.3 m²
29. 2.2 m²
30. 14 m
31. 13 m
32. 9.6 m²
33. 12.8 m²
34. 41.3 m²

Mind Boggler

7 Volume, Capacity and Mass

1. 24
2. 18
3. 28
4. 36
5. 900 cm³ ; 150 cm³ ; 3000 cm³
6. 900 mL ; 150 mL ; 3000 mL
7. 3 L
8. 20
9. 6 times
10. 25 cm x 25 cm x 20 cm
11. 12500 cm³
12. 40 m³
13. 80 boxes
14. 100 ; 100
15. 250
16. 5 ; 30 ; 30 ; 4500 ; 4500
17. kilogram
18. tonne
19. gram
20. kilogram
21. tonne
22. 4.4
23. 200
24. 20
25. 1.6
26. 250
27. 400
28. 1500
29. 1.50
30a. 20 000 cm³
b. 8000 cm³
c. 1875 cm³
31. 576 cm³
32. 3 cm x 3 cm x 4 cm
33. 36 cm³
34. 40 g
35a. 25 slices
b. 25 000 slices
36a. 4000 cm³
b. 500 cm³

Mind Boggler

3

Progress Test

1.
```
  5984
+ 2079
  8063
- 3475
  4588
```

2.
```
    53
x   69
   477
  3180
  3657
```

3.
```
    76
x   98
   608
  6840
  7448
```

4.
```
      787
8 )6296
      56
      69
      64
      56
      56
```

5. 3
6. 54
7. 11
8. 0.57
9. 0.79
10. 0.38
11. >
12. <
13. <
14. 13.21
15. 4.19
16. 50.56

17.
```
    0.79
8 )6.32
    56
    72
    72
```

18. 1593
19. 0.608
20. 780
21. 300
22. 1700
23. 3200
24. 1200
25. 2700
26. 1600
27. 1200
28. 7
29. 10
30. 9
31. 12
32. 32 cm ; 64 cm²
33. 12.6 cm ; 9.2 cm²
34. 16 m ; 13 m²
35. 1701 cm³
36. 1960 m³
37. 1500 cm³
38. 11 : 59 : 04
39. May 16
40. C
41. D
42. C
43. B
44. B
45. D
46. B
47. A
48. B
49. D

50a. 30 x 50 x 20 = 30 000
The volume of water is 30 000 cm³.
b. 30 x 50 x 5 = 7500
The volume of the stones is 7500 cm³.
c. 30 x 50 x 40 = 60 000
60 000 cm³ = 60 000 mL = 60 L
The capacity of the aquarium is 60 L.

51a. 17 x 18 + 3 x 15 = 306 + 45 = 351
351 students can be seated in the hall.
b. 360 – 351 = 9 ; 9 students have to stand.
c. 360 ÷ 20 = 36 ÷ 2 = 18
There are 18 teachers in the hall.
d. 11 h 7 min – 9 h 15 min = 1 h 52 min
The assembly lasts for 1 h 52 min.

8 Angles and 2-D Figures

1. 90° ; 45° ; 120° ; 180° ; 75° ; 150°
2. Right ; Acute ; Obtuse ; Straight ; Acute ; Obtuse

3. 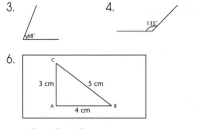 4. 5.

6.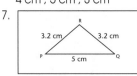
90° ; 37° ; 53°
4 cm ; 5 cm ; 3 cm

7.
40° ; 40°
3.2 cm ; 3.2 cm

8. Scalene ; Isosceles
9. Right-angled ; Obtuse-angled

11.-12. (Suggested answers)
10. 11. 12.

13. F
14. E
15. A
16. B
17. 5
18. 3
19. 7

20.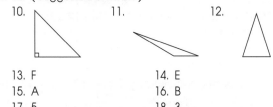
0
21. 1
22. 2
23. 4

24.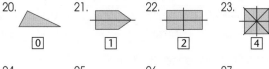
1
25. 0
26. 3
27. 1

28.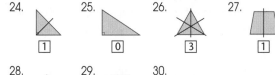
4
29. 0
30. 0

31.-32. (Suggested answers)
31.
32. 3 cm ; 3 cm ; 2 cm ; 2 cm

33. Octagon
34. Rectangle
35. Pentagon
36. Triangle

37.-39.
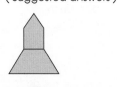 yellow 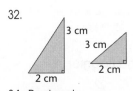 red

37.
38.
39.

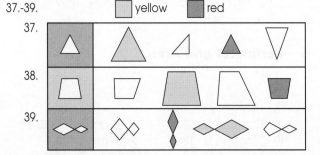

76

40.-42. (Suggested answers)

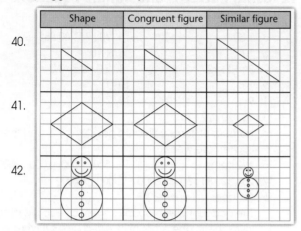

	Shape	Congruent figure	Similar figure
40.			
41.			
42.			

Mind Boggler

14

9 3-D Figures

1. Square
2. 6
3. Rectangle
4. 5 ; Triangle, Rectangle
5. Cone, Cylinder
6. Circle
7. 8
8. 12
9. 3
10. Cube, Rectangular prism, Rectangular pyramid
11. A ; B ; E
12. 4 ; 5 ; 6 ; 7
13. 6 ; 8 ; 10 ; 12
14. 4 ; 5 ; 6 ; 7
15. 3 ; 4 ; 5 ; 6
16. Triangle ; Rectangle ; Pentagon ; Hexagon
17. vertices ; faces
18. triangular faces
19. edges
20. 1
21. A ; B ; D
22. Tetrahedron or Triangular pyramid
23. Cube
24. Sphere
25. Cylinder
26. Hexagonal pyramid
27. Triangular prism
28. Rectangular prism
29. Cube
30. Rectangular prism
31. Triangular prism
32. Square pyramid
33. Tetrahedron or Triangular pyramid
34. Tetrahedron
35. Cone
36. Cube
37. Triangular prism
38. Rectangular prism

	Top view	Front view	Side view
39.			
40.			
41.			
42.			

Mind Boggler

stick

The common base of the two triangular pyramids is also a triangle.

10 Coordinates and Transformations

1.-8.
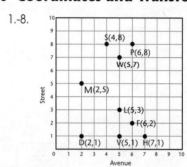

7. (5, 1)
8. (5, 7)
9. Museum and Doctor's office
10. Food court
11. Park
12. School
13. Library

14. 15. 16.
17. 18. 19.
20. 21. 22.

23. 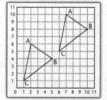 24.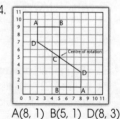
A(2, 6) B(5, 4) C(1, 1)   A(8, 1) B(5, 1) D(8, 3)

25.
A(7,1) B(10, 4) C(4, 3) D(5, 1)
26. Translation
27. Reflection
28. Rotation
29. Translation
30. Reflection
31. Reflection
32. Translation
33. ✔
34. ✔
35.

36. ✔

37.

38. ✔

39. A, F, I

40. B, D, E

Mind Boggler

1.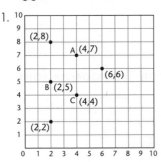

2. (6, 6), (2, 2) or (2, 8)

11 Patterns

1.    2.

3.    4.

5.

6. 9 ; 11 ; 13   7. 16 ; 32 ; 64
8. 15 ; 21 ; 28   9. 4 ; 2 ; 0
10. 11 ; 6 ; 0   11. 100 ; 50 ; 25
12. 11 116 ; 111 116 ; 1 111 116
13. Each number is five more than the previous number.
14. Each number is twice the previous number.
15. Each number is seven less than the previous number.
16. Each number is half of the previous number.
17. K ; P ; V   18. Q ; W
19. R ; X   20. Y
21. LET'S GO TO A MOVIE TONIGHT.
22. WHICH MOVIE DO YOU WANT TO SEE?
23. 7 ; 8 ; 10   24. 22 ; 32 ; 31
25. 70 ; 60 ; 55   26. 34 ; 30 ; 36
27. 30 ; 50 ; 40   28. 14 ; 28 ; 26
29.-32. (Suggested answers for number pairs in the tables)
29. 6, 18 ; 7, 21 ; Multiply the 1st number by 3.
30. 10, 5 ; 22, 11 ; Divide the 1st number by 2.
31. 3, 5 ; 6, 11 ; Multiply the 1st number by 2. Then subtract 1.
32. 8, 5 ; 12, 7 ; Divide the 1st number by 2. Then add 1.
33.

34. 9 ; 11 ; 13 ; 15 ; 17   35. 21
36. 13
37. The number of toothpicks goes up by 2 each time.
38. The number of toothpicks is obtained by multiplying the number of triangles by 2. Then add 1.

Mind Boggler

1. 6.25   2. 6.25   3. No

12 Using Patterns and Simple Equations

1. 50 ; 60 ; 70 ; 80 ; 90   2. 9
3. 1.30   4. 70 ; 75 ; 80 ; 85 ; 90
5. 10   6. 1.10
7. 8 ; 10 ; 12   8. 2.0 ; 2.5 ; 3.0
9. 16   10. 12
11. 9   12. 4
13. 16 ; 20 ; 22 ; 26
14. Number of items collected goes up by 2, and then 4 in alternate weeks.
15. 122 items   16. 500 ; 1000 ; 2000 ; 4000
17. 26 ; 32 ; 38 ; 3000 ; 6000 ; 12 000 ; 24 000
18. (Suggested answer)
    The account which doubles every 5 years is a better investment. The amount invested grows 8 times in 18 years if it doubles every 6 years whilst it needs only 15 years to grow 8 times if it doubles every 5 years.
19. 60 ; 65
20. Mass of Gerry increases by 5 g and then 10 g in alternate weeks.
21. Week 9
22. (Suggested answer)
    No. Its mass is 35 g at week 2, but it is only 50 g at week 4.
23a. 5 min 12 s   b. The 7th day
24a. 6 min 40 s   b. The 7th lap
25a. 2.7 m   b. On day 11
26. 1.46 m   b. On the 9th attempt
27. 9   28. 28
29. 10   30. 2
31. 116   32. 30
33. 20   34. 50
35. 90   36. 34
37. 92   38. 0.5
39. 0.1   40. 0.01
41. 10   42. 2
43. 1.2   44. 0.1
45. 1.4   46. 5.9
47. 11.2   48. 5
49. 100   50. 10
51. 6   52. 96
53. 12   54. B
55. C   56. A

Mind Boggler

30

13 Data and Graphs

1. American   2. Japanese
3. Korean   4. 15
5. 30   6. 45
7. 20   8. 75
9. Japanese
10a. American   b. Japanese
    c. Korean   d. European
11. Hockey   12. Tennis
13. 4   14. 19
15. 6   16. 6

17. 3
18. 30
19. 45
20. $\frac{2}{9}$
21. $\frac{1}{4}$
22. Bar graph
23. 65 000
24. 130 000
25. 1989
26. 8000
27. 60 000
28. 1975-1980
29. 1985-1990
30. The population in Bellfield will be about 145 000 in 2005. From the graph, the increase in population between 1980 and 2000 was about 60 000, so the increase for every five years is about 15 000.
31. Line graph. It can show the trend of the population growth.
32. 1.4 ; 2.4 ; 5.4
33. 1 ; 2 ; 5
34. 2
35. 1.6 ; 2

Mind Boggler

4

14 Probability

1.
    Tuna (T)   — PT
    Egg (E)   — PE
    Cheese (C) — PC
    Tuna (T)   — ST
    Egg (E)   — SE
    Cheese (C) — SC

2. 6
3. $\frac{3}{6}$ or $\frac{1}{2}$
4. $\frac{2}{6}$ or $\frac{1}{3}$
5. $\frac{1}{6}$
6. $\frac{9}{10}$
7. $\frac{1}{100}$
8. $\frac{1}{10}$
9. Green
10. Black and White
11. $\frac{1}{4}$
12. $\frac{1}{2}$
13. $\frac{3}{4}$
14. 75 times
15.

+	1	2	3	4	5	6
1	2	3	4	5	6	7
2	3	4	5	6	7	8
3	4	5	6	7	8	9
4	5	6	7	8	9	10
5	6	7	8	9	10	11
6	7	8	9	10	11	12

16. 36
17. 11
18. 7 ; $\frac{6}{36}$ or $\frac{1}{6}$
19. 2 ; 12 ; $\frac{1}{36}$
20. 5
21. $\frac{5}{12}$
22. A boy
23. $\frac{3}{4}$
24. $\frac{1}{4}$
25. $\frac{1}{6}$
26. No
27. $\frac{4}{5}$

28. $\frac{3}{7}$
29. $\frac{1}{9}$
30. $\frac{1}{5}$
31. $\frac{5}{12}$
32. $\frac{2}{3}$
33. $\frac{7}{12}$
34. $\frac{3}{4}$
35. 0
36. Yes
37. No
38. No

Mind Boggler

1. $\frac{1}{2}$
2. 0
3. 1

Final Test

1. D
2. C
3. B
4. C
5. B.
6. C
7. A
8. C
9. B
10. B
11. B
12. A
13. C
14. D
15. A
16. B
17. A
18. D
19. B
20. D
21. C
22. A
23. C
24. D
25. B
26. A
27. B
28. A
29. C
30. C
31. Number of seats : 15 x 13 = 195
    Number of people standing : 200 – 195 = 5
    5 people are standing.
32a. Try : 1.29 x 8 = 10.32 ; 1.29 x 7 = 9.03
     She can get 7 books.
   b. Change : 10 – 9.03 = 0.97
     She can get $ 0.97 change.
33.

```
        854
    7 )5982
        56
        38
        35
         32
         28
          4
```

The remainder is 4.
Check : 854 x 7 + 4 = 5978 + 4 = 5982
34. Approx. amount of water displaced : 580 – 250 = 330
    1 mL = 1 cm³
    Volume of the rock is about 330 cm³.
35a. He earns : 10.50 x 9 x 5 = 472.50
     He earns $472.50 per week.
   b. His hourly wage on Sunday : 78.75 ÷ 5 = 15.75
     His hourly wage on Sunday was $15.75.
   C. He earned : 78.75 + 472.50 = 551.25
     He earned $551.25 last week.

36.
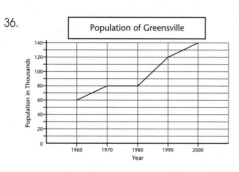

D.
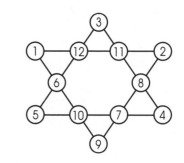

37. 1980 to 1990   38. 1970

39. 80 000

40. It can show the tendency of the growth of population.

41. 9 ; 2 ; 4 ; 5 ; 6 ; 4   42. 30 cars

43. $\frac{1}{5}$ 44. $\frac{1}{6}$

45. $\frac{4}{15}$ 46. $\frac{7}{10}$

47. 54   48. 50

49. 48   50. No

51. 30   52. 67.5

53. (Answer may vary)   54. $1

55. 250   56. 300

57. $\frac{1}{2}$ 58. $\frac{1}{6}$

59. 150   60. $\frac{3}{11}$

61. 25   62. 450

63. $110

64.-65. (Suggested answers)

64a. Basketball   b. Hockey

c. Baseball   d. Football

65a. Basketball   b. Hockey

c. Baseball   d. Football

E. (Suggested answer)

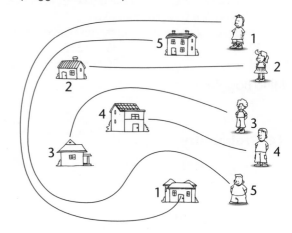

F.

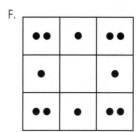

Game Cards

A. (Suggested answer)

B.

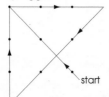

C.

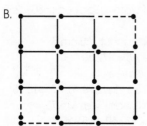